FORGOTTEN

AMONG THE

LILIES

FORGOTTEN

AMONG THE

LILIES

Learning to Live Beyond Our Fears

RONALD ROLHEISER

GALILEE/DOUBLEDAY
New York   London   Toronto   Sydney   Auckland

A GALILEE BOOK
PUBLISHED BY DOUBLEDAY
a division of Random House, Inc.

GALILEE and DOUBLEDAY are registered trademarks of Random House,
Inc., and the portrayal of a ship with a cross above a book is a
trademark of Random House, Inc.

A hardcover edition of this book was published in 2004 by Doubleday.

Book design by Ruth Lee-Mui

The Library of Congress has cataloged the hardcover edition as follows:

Rolheiser, Ronald.
Forgotten among the lilies / Ronald Rolheiser.
p. cm.
1. Spirituality—Catholic Church. 2. Spiritual life—Catholic Church.
3. Christian life—Catholic authors. I. Title.

BX2350.65.R647 2005
248—dc22   2004061835

ISBN 0-385-51232-5

I abandoned and forgot myself
. . . .

Leaving my cares
Forgotten among the lilies.

ST. JOHN OF THE CROSS,
The Dark Night of the Soul

CONTENTS

PREFACE

THOMAS MERTON, journeying during an extended period of solitude, wrote:

> It is enough to be, in an ordinary human mode, with one's hunger and sleep, one's cold and warmth, rising and going to bed. Putting on blankets and taking them off, making coffee and then drinking it. Defrosting the refrigerator, reading, meditating, working, praying. I live as my ancestors have lived on this earth, until eventually I die. Amen. There is no need to make an assertion of my life, especially about it as mine, though doubtless it is not somebody else's. I must learn gradually to forget program and artifice. (Quoted in J. H. Griffin, *Follow the Ecstasy*, Latitudes Press, 1983)

Rarely is life enough for us. Rarely are we able to live restfully the spirit of our own lives. Most often what, where, and how we are living seem small, insignificant, petty and depressingly domestic. We seldom notice our hunger and sleep, cold and warmth. Rarely do we taste the coffee we drink. Instead we go through our days too preoccupied, too compulsive, too driven and too dissatisfied to really be able to be present to and celebrate our own lives. Always, it seems, we are somehow missing out on life.

Added to this restlessness is fear and guilt. We live always in fear—about losing life, losing health, losing loved ones, losing a job, losing securities, losing youth, losing respect and losing ourselves. As well, our lives are always colored by guilt—guilt about things we have done wrong, guilt about things we have not done at all, and guilt, at times, simply about being alive, healthy and experiencing life's pleasures.

For very few of us is human life a simple endeavor. Most of us understand only too clearly what St. Paul meant when he said, "For now we see as through a glass, darkly." We live as in an enigma, always partially away from home, longing to understand more fully and to be understood more fully. Slowly we tire of pilgrimage. We want to go home.

This book is a series of reflections which attempt, from many perspectives, to shed some light upon these problems. In essence they attempt to help a pilgrim home.

Margaret Atwood has said: "What touches you is what you touch." Accordingly these reflections touch on a whole lot of things, stuff of all kinds: restlessness, inconsummation, innocence and its loss, guilt and reconciliation, patience and chastity, death and loss, God's unconditional love, passion, friendship, love, sex, romance, community, social problems, human complexity and resiliency, weakness and depression, sin and conversion, the Eucharist, prayer and the obscurity and monasticism of daily life.

The title *Forgotten among the Lilies* is the final line in John of the Cross's poem *The Dark Night of the Soul*. In that poem John traces our spiritual journey and shows how it is meant to end up in a freedom that allows us to live beyond the obsessions, restlessness, fears and guilts that rob us of the spirit of our own lives, of the feel of our own cold and warmth, of the taste of our own coffee and of the consolation of God.

This book is for those who struggle to make this life,

such as it is, enough. It is for those who ache to be outside themselves, with their headaches and heartaches *forgotten among the lilies*. It is dedicated to those who struggle with restlessness, guilt and obsessions, who struggle to taste their own coffee and who struggle to feel the consolation of God.

ACKNOWLEDGMENTS

MANY PERSONS have contributed to this book. I need to thank especially, however, my family, who always support me; the Oblates of St. Mary's province, who always trust me; Newman Theological College in Edmonton, which always gives me a job, an altar, a classroom, a desk and a salary; as well as the *Western Catholic Reporter* and the *Catholic Herald*, which originally published many of these reflections. I want too to thank in a special way Delia Smith for initially, and continually, promoting my writings in England. Finally a huge thanks to everyone at Hodder & Stoughton, especially to Juliet Newport, who originally suggested this book and whose hand guided it to completion.

RONALD ROLHEISER, OMI

FORGOTTEN

AMONG THE

LILIES

I

RESTLESSNESS, SPIRIT AND THE MARTYRDOM OF OBSCURITY

The only hope, or else despair
Lies in the choice of pyre or pyre—
To be redeemed from fire by fire.

Who then devised the torment? Love.
Love is the unfamiliar Name
Behind the hands that wove
The intolerable shirt of flame,
Which human power cannot remove.
 We only live, only suspire
 Consumed by either fire or fire.
     (T. S. ELIOT, *Four Quartets*)

Restless Hearts Yearn for God

WE ARE FIRED into life by a madness that comes from our incompleteness. We awake to life tense, aching, erotic, full of sex and restlessness.

This dis-ease is, singularly, the most important force within existence. It is the force for love and we are fundamentally shaped by our loves and deformed by their distortions.

Shakespeare called this our "immortal longings" and poets, philosophers, and mystics have always recognized that, within it, there is precisely something of immortality.

Religiously, we have surrounded this longing with chastity and mystique.

Ultimately our restless aching was seen as nothing less than the yearning within us for God. Augustine's interpretation of this eros was seen as the proper one: "You have made us for yourself, Lord, and our hearts are restless until they rest in you."

The longing was understood religiously: Adam, missing his rib, longing for Eve, man and woman, woman and man, longing for a primal wholeness in God and each other. This was high longing, eros as the spark of the divine in us, the fire from the anvil of God imprisoned inside us like a skylark, causing hopeless disquiet!

In the light of such divine restlessness we lived as pilgrims in time, longing for a consummation in a kingdom not fully of this world, caught, in Karl Rahner's words, "in the torment of the insufficiency of everything attainable, inconsummate, but knowing that here in this life all symphonies remain unfinished."

In such a view, we pursued each other, embraced each other, and loved and made love to each other against the horizon of the infinite, under a high symbolic hedge. Love, romance, sex, and passion were sacred things, surrounded by much chastity and mystique.

Today that hedge is lower, the mystique and the chastity are less. We no longer embrace against the horizon of the infinite and our aches are no longer seen as longing for the transcendent.

Instead, for the most part, we have trivialized this longing, making it mean something much more concrete. The longing is for the good life, for good sex, for good successes, for what everybody else has, for the sweetening of life.

There is little mystique in this. Plato, in his Symposium, tells of his students sitting around "telling wonderful stories of the meaning of their longing." Mystics, in their writings, tell of their deep longing for consummation within the body of Christ.

Today we rarely sit around and tell wonderful stories of the meaning of our longing, and, ordinarily, there is little talk of aching for consummation within the body of Christ.

Our stories are, for the most part, of yearnings more concretely channeled. It is a rare self-understanding today which lets one believe that his or her aches and yearnings are mystical. We are not accustomed to think in such high terms, our symbols are more humble.

Our aches and longings are seen as directed toward what we can attain, practically, in the here and now, achievement, success, sex, limited love and enjoyment.

There is nothing bad about these things, but, in the end, if we define our deepest longings as directed toward them in themselves, we end up in despair. Eventually, we no longer believe that we can recover a primal wholeness through the embrace of another, the perpetuity of our seed, and the contemplation of God. We lower our sights. We trivialize our longing.

We no longer see our longing as a congenital and holy restlessness put in us by God to push us toward the infinite. Instead it becomes a tamed and tame thing, domesticated, anesthetized and distracted. We are restless only in a tired way (which drains us of energy) and not in a divine way (which gives us energy).

And so we should ask ourselves the question: What kind of lovers are we?

Are we still fired into life by a madness which lets us understand the insatiability of our hearts as a call to infinite love? Do we still see ourselves as pursuing each other, embracing each other, and loving each other against the horizon of the infinite? Do we still understand ourselves as meeting on holy ground with all the mystique and chastity that this implies?

Or, do we believe that life is best lived without such mysticism, high romance, high eros, and high chastity? Do we still tell each other wonderful stories of the meaning of our longings or do we discourage each other from raising our eyes above the immediate?

Do we cry with each other and support each other in the frustration of our incompleteness or do we give each other the impression that there is something wrong with us because our lives are inconsummate and our symphonies are incomplete?

Do we still take our longings and emptiness to God in prayer or do we demand that life gives us, here and now, the full symphony?

Do we lovingly and gratefully receive the spirit of our own lives, despite the tensions, or do we live in angry jealousy?

Are we loving against an infinite horizon or is our eros directed only towards the concrete sweetening of life?

What kind of lovers are we?

Longing Is Our Spiritual Lot

ON FEBRUARY 12TH, 1944, thirteen-year-old Anne Frank wrote the following words in her now famous Diary (Pan, 1968):

> Today the sun is shining, the sky is a deep blue, there is a lovely breeze and I am longing—so longing—for everything. To talk, for freedom, for friends, to be alone.
>
> And I do so long . . . to cry! I feel as if I am going to burst, and I know that it would get better with crying; but I can't, I'm restless, I go from room to room, breathe through the crack of a closed window, feel my heart beating, as if it is saying, "can't you satisfy my longing at last?"
>
> I believe that it is spring within me, I feel that spring is awakening, I feel it in my whole body and soul. It is an effort to behave normally, I feel utterly confused. I don't know what to read, what to write, what to do, I only know that I am longing.

There is in all of us, at the very center of our lives, a tension, an aching, a burning in the heart that is insatiable, non-quietable and very deep. Sometimes we experience this longing as focused on a person, particularly if we are in a love that is not consummated. Other times we experience this yearning as a longing to attain something.

Most often, though, it is a longing without a clear name or focus, an aching that cannot be clearly pinpointed or described. Like Anne Frank, we only know that we are restless, full of disquiet, aching at a level that we cannot seem to get at.

When we look into history, philosophy, poetry, mysticism and literature we see an astonishing variety of ways in which this aching is expressed.

For instance, many of us have read Richard Bach's little parable, *Jonathan Livingston Seagull*. This book spoke deeply to millions of people. It is a very simple story: Jonathan is a seagull who, when he comes to consciousness, is not satisfied with being a seagull. He looks at his life, and the lives of other seagulls, and he finds it too small: "All a seagull ever does is eat and fight!" So Jonathan tries to burst out. He tries to fly higher, to fly faster, to do anything that might break the asphyxiating limits of being a seagull. He does not know what he wants, he only knows that he is hopelessly restless, that he must break out. Many times he crashes and almost kills himself, but he keeps trying.

This is a story obviously more of the human heart than of a seagull. It describes our search, our aching, our congenital propensity for the limitless, the free, the total embrace.

In more abstract ways, this has been expressed in history: Philosophers speak of "a desire of the part to return to the whole"; mystics speak of "the spark of the divine in us"; the ancient Greeks spoke of something they called *nostos*, homesickness (a feeling of never being at home, even when you are at home).

The Vikings called it "wanderlust," the insatiable need to push further and further into the horizon; Shakespeare talked of "immortal longings"; Gerard Manley Hopkins called the human spirit "an imprisoned skylark"; Augustine prayed to God: "You have made us for yourself, Lord, and our hearts are restless until they rest in you"; e. e. cummings, poet, said: "For every mile the feet go, the heart goes nine."

All of these feelings are in all of us. We are all deeply and hopelessly subject to dis-ease, incapable in this life of finding lasting rest. This restlessness, however, must never be seen as something which sets us against what is spiritual, religious and of God.

In fact this hopeless aching and lack of ease is the very basis of the spiritual life. What we do with the eros inside us, be it heroic or perverse, is our spiritual life.

The tragedy is that so many persons, full of riches and bursting with life, see this drive as something which is essentially irreligious, as something which sets them against what is spiritual. Nothing could be further from the truth. Our erotic impulses are God's lure in us. They are our spirit!

We experience them precisely as "spirit," as soul, as that which makes us more than mere animals. Our soul is not an invisible kind of tissue floating around within us, that stains when we sin and cleanses when we are in grace and which ultimately floats away from the body after death. Our soul is our eros, our minds and hearts in their deep restlessness.

Living the tension that arises out of that is the spiritual life. In that sense, everyone has a spiritual life—either a good one or a destructive one. Our spirits make it impossible for us to be static, we must move outside ourselves.

That movement outward (which is experienced as a double tension: a hunger which drives us outward and an attractive outside person or object which draws us outward) is either beneficial to us or destructive. When it is beneficial, we have a good spiritual life; when it is destructive, we have a bad one.

It is important, therefore, that we do not identify the spiritual life with something which is exotic (for religious fanatics), extraordinary (for professional contemplatives), or as something which is not for those who are full-blooded and full of eros.

It is non-negotiable. If you are alive, you are restless, full of spirit. What you do with that spirit is your spiritual life.

The Martyrdom of Obscurity

WE CRAVE FEW THINGS as deeply as self-expression.

Deep within the eros that makes us restless and dissatisfied lies the incurable need to express ourselves, to be known,
recognized, understood, and seen by others as unique and as
having deep riches inside us.

Self-expression, being known and being experienced in
our depth, is vital to living and loving. A heart which is unknown, unappreciated in its depth and lacking in meaningful
self-expression is always a restless and frustrated heart. It is
normally, too, a competitive and bitter one. But meaningful
self-expression is difficult and full self-expression is impossible.

In the end all of us live in obscurity, unknown, frustrated.
Our lives are always smaller than our needs and our dreams.
Ultimately we all live in small towns, no matter where we
live; and save for a few brief moments of satisfaction, spend
most of our lives waiting for a fuller moment to come, waiting for a time when we will be less hidden.

From this frustration stems a tremendous restlessness
and dissatisfaction. Each of us would like to be the famous
writer, the graceful ballerina, the admired athlete, the movie
star, the cover girl, the renowned scholar, the Nobel prize
winner, the household name. But in the end each of us is just
another unknown, living with other unknowns, collecting an
occasional autograph.

Our lives always seem too small for us. We sense ourselves as extraordinary persons living very ordinary lives. Because of this sense of obscurity we are seldom satisfied, easeful and happy with our lives.

There is always, too, much still inside us that wants expression, that needs recognition, that feels that something very precious, unique and rich is living and dying in futility.

And in truth, seen only from the perspective of this world, much that is precious, unique and rich is living and dying in futility. Only a rare few achieve meaningful self-expression. There is a certain martyrdom in this. Iris Murdoch has said: "Art has its martyrs, not the least of which are those who have preserved their silence." Lack of self-expression, whether chosen or imposed by circumstances, is a real death.

Like all death, however, it can be *paschal* or *terminal*. If merely accepted as inevitable it leads to bitterness and a broken spirit. If linked to the paschal mystery of Christ, if it is seen as an opportunity to enter the hidden life of Christ, it leads to a new ease in life, to restfulness; and it lays the ax to the root of our competitiveness, anger and bitterness.

Today we are called as Christians to the martyrdom of obscurity. Christianity always invites its adherents to martyrdom. To be a follower of Christ demands that one lay down one's life. But this takes various forms.

For Jesus and his apostles, as for many early Christians during the times of the persecutions, martyrdom meant physical death. They had to give up the possibilities that this life offered in order to remain true to a more distant possibility—permanent intimacy with God and each other. In dying they entered the hidden life of Christ.

That type of martyrdom is still being asked of Christians in many parts of the world, notably in Latin America.

In North America and Western Europe, however, at least of many of us, a different kind of martyrdom is being asked.

Our culture persecutes its Christians in a different way. Affluence and leisure have created a higher psychic temperature. These have focused us on interpersonal, sexual, artistic, athletic and scientific achievement. In a word, they have focused us on self-expression. In our culture meaningful self-expression is everything; lack of it is death. Yet it is this death that paschally we must enter.

Not that we should, in the name of the Gospel, be uncreative, unresourceful, phlegmatic or stoic underachievers. But we should, in the name of the Gospel, enter the hidden life of Christ within which that current of eros which drives us mercilessly toward self-expression can be more properly channeled, so that we do not go through life unhealthily competitive, bitter, angry, hopelessly restless, not at ease, and basically unhappy because we are ordinary and obscure.

Only when we enter the martyrdom of obscurity will our ordinary lives be enough.

Thomas Merton, after several years in a hermitage, wrote: "It is enough to be, in an ordinary human mode . . . I must learn to live so as gradually to forget programme and artifice."

Ordinary life can be enough for us, but only if we first undergo the martyrdom of obscurity and enter Christ's hidden life. It is not easy, however. In many ways it is easier to sacrifice life itself than to sacrifice dreams.

Staying Home on a Friday Night

I AM OLD ENOUGH to have known another time. Things were different when I was little. Many of life's pleasures were not available and people made do, celebrating what there was to celebrate and not over-expecting. Back then few expected or demanded the whole pie. Heaven was seen as something for later.

My parents and their generation lived a simple spiritual philosophy: This life is but a short time of waiting, "mourning and weeping in a vale of tears!" It is not so important to be happy.

Today there are sneers about their tears. But that somber philosophy of theirs got them through life with their faith and loves intact and, ironically, probably equipped them with a greater capacity for enjoyment and happiness than we possess today.

There is today too little talk, in our churches and in our world, about the "vale of tears" and the incompleteness of our present lives.

Spiritualities of the resurrection and psychologies of self-actualization, whatever their other strengths, no longer give us permission to be in pain, to be unwhole, ill, unattractive, aged, unfulfilled or even just alone on a Friday night.

The idea is all too present that we can only be happy if we somehow fulfill every hunger within us, if our lives are completely whole, consummated and we are never alone on a Friday night. Unless every pleasure that we yearn for can be tasted we cannot be happy.

Because of this we over-expect. We stand before life and love in a greedy posture and with unrealistic expectations, demanding the resolution of all our eros and tension. However life in this world can never give us that.

We are pilgrims on earth, exiles journeying toward home. The world is passing away. We have God's word for it. And we need God's word for it! Too much in our experience today militates against the fact that here in this life all symphonies remain unfinished.

Somehow we have come to believe that a final solution for the burning tensions within us lies within our present grasp. I am not sure who or what gives us this idea. Maybe it is the movie and television industries with their leading men and leading ladies who are presented to us as already redeemed, persons who are gorgeous, immersed in love and meaning, and who have the wherewithal within their grasp to taste whatever life has to offer.

But something has led us to the belief that we need not put up with tension and frustration and that there are persons in this life who are already enjoying a redeemed life.

That belief, however unconscious and unexpressed, lies at the root of much of our restlessness and unhappiness today. None of us is whole, not even our gorgeous leading men and ladies. Yet because we believe that somehow we can or should be whole, we go through life denigrating what chances we have for rest and happiness.

A simple example serves to illustrate: In our culture we suffer from what might be termed "Friday night syndrome." Few people can stay home quietly and rest on a Friday night. Why? Is it because we are not tired and ideally could not ap-

preciate a nice quiet time? No! We cannot stay home quietly
on a Friday night because inside us moves a restless demon
that assures us that everyone in the whole world is doing
something exciting on Friday night. Once that voice is heard,
then our homes, our families and our commitments begin to
look unexciting. Peace and restfulness slip away and we are
caught up in an insatiable restlessness.

This example illustrates the basic principle: So much of
our unhappiness comes from comparing our lives, our friendships, our loves, our commitments, our duties, our bodies and
our sexuality to some idealized and non-Christian vision of
things which falsely assures us that there is a heaven on earth.

When that happens, and it does, our tensions begin to
drive us mad, in this case to a cancerous restlessness.

In a culture (and, at times, in a church) that tells us that
no happiness is possible unless every ache and restlessness inside us is fulfilled, how hard it is to be happy.

How tragic it is to be alone! How tragic it is to be unmarried! How tragic it is to be married, but not completely fulfilled romantically and sexually! How tragic it is not to be
good-looking! How tragic it is to be unhealthy, aged, handicapped! How tragic it is to be caught up in duties and commitments, small children and diapers and routine, which
limit our freedom and relationships! How tragic it is to be
poor! How tragic it is to go through life and not be able to
taste every pleasure on earth! It almost isn't worth living!

There is wisdom and, yes, even comfort, in the old
"mourning and weeping in this vale of tears" philosophy.
Sometimes that expression was abused and people forgot
that the Creator did not just make us for life after death. He
did also intend some life after birth!

But those who lived that philosophy generally did not attempt to milk life for more than it could give them. Those

who lived that philosophy were a lot less restless and greedy for experience than we are today.

They could much more restfully enjoy God's great gifts—life, love, youth, health, friendship and sexuality—even as they are limitedly given in this life. Those who lived that philosophy were, I am sure, much more restful on Friday nights!

God Beats Small-Time Blues

SIGMUND FREUD stated that neurosis is the disease of the normal person and that everyone is neurotic to some degree. This is true if one defines neurosis as he did, simply as meaning that one suffers more than one needs to. Neurosis, for him, is more a dis-ease than a disease.

For Freud, this dis-ease comes about because of the repression of sex. In his understanding we are so hopelessly and incurably sexed, with such limited access for sexual expression, that we are forced to repress most of our erotic energies. Eventually these repressed energies dominate and preoccupy our lives in a negative way. Everyone, subsequently, lives in a fundamental dis-ease.

There is certainly some truth in that.

More recently thinkers such as Martin Heidegger and Ernest Becker have argued that we are all neurotic, but have suggested that the root of our dis-ease is not so much repressed sexuality as the repression of our fear of death. For them, we have a deep sense of our own mortality and, consciously and unconsciously, repress it. Eventually this causes a neurosis which robs us of the full joy of living because we are afraid of dying. Again, obviously, there is much truth in this.

More recently still a number of psychologists and novelists, among others, have suggested that there is a different reason why we are fundamentally dis-eased. For them, while repressed sexuality and fear of death certainly unsettle our

lives and cause untold restlessness, they are not the real reason why our lives are seldom peaceful and contented. They
submit that our neurotic restlessness has another cause.

In our western world we live in a culture that stresses the
importance and significance of the individual, while at the
same time downplaying the importance of God. These two
emphases, the significance of the individual life and the absence of God, cannot go together without creating an intolerable restlessness inside each of us.

A fundamental dis-ease results when the truths that are
revealed by God are taught in a world that postures indepen-
dence of God.

What happens when we are raised to believe that we are,
each of us, precious, special and meant to leave a lasting
mark on this earth . . . and we live in a world in which we
are obscure, unknown, homogenized, taken for granted and
deprived of meaningful self-expression?

What happens when we are taught that our lives have
deep significance and that our personalities, our dreams, our
pains, our joys, and our loves have infinite importance . . .
and we live in a world which cannot give us this sense?

What happens inside us when we sense how precious are
our individual stories, in all their unique intricacies, and we
live in a world which is not interested in our stories and is
bored when we begin to speak of ourselves?

What happens when we are told by our world that our
daydreams are true and that we are infinitely precious, but
that same world, precisely because it no longer relies on God
to give us that preciousness, cannot offer us a sense of specialness?

What happens? In brief, we get very restless. We become
deeply and hopelessly dissatisfied. The joys that our lives do
give us tend to pale and be insignificant because we feel that

they, and we, are small-time, small-town, obscure, too little known and recognized.

We end up frustrated, feeling trapped in a domesticity that excludes us from where we would like to be and from whom we would like to be with. Our families and friends do not satisfy us because they, like ourselves, seem small-time. They are too much like us to be of help in our restlessness. We crave relationships with the famous, the powerful, the achievers, with those who have attained significance in the world's eyes and whose stories the world deems precious and interesting.

We become obsessed with the need for self-expression, with the need for achieving something that is unique and lasting. We fear dying without leaving a permanent mark.

Our daily lives seem poor and uninteresting, and we live so much of our lives waiting, waiting for someone or something or some moment to come along and give us significance and preciousness.

Our world teaches us that we are significant and precious, but then deprives us of the one thing that can make us so, God. This sets off an incurable ache.

A sense of our individual significance and a lack of a sense of God cannot go together without creating a restless and intolerable dis-ease.

Only God can give us the sense of our own preciousness and ultimate significance. Only in a life rooted deeply in prayer, where we can live contentedly hidden in Christ and, there, accept the martyrdom of obscurity, will our aching and dissatisfaction cease and our dis-ease give way to restful contentment.

Leaving God's Mark

We nurse within our hearts the hope that we are different, that we are special, that we are extraordinary. We long for the assurance that our birth was no accident, that a god had a hand in our coming to be, that we exist by divine fiat. We ache for a cure for the ultimate disease of mortality. Our madness comes when the pressure is too great and we fabricate a vital lie to cover up the fact that we are mediocre, accidental, mortal. We fail to see the glory of the Good News. The vital lie is unnecessary because all the things we truly long for have been freely given us. (Alan Jones, *Journey into Christ*, SPCK, 1978)

ALL OF US, I am sure, know what is meant by those words. On the one hand we sense that we are extraordinary, creatures under divine providence, precious and significant, irrespective of our practical fortunes in life.

We sense that we are not mere evolutionary accidents, simple victims of fate, chance, luck, randomness and accident, doomed to disappear for ever. Deep down there is the feeling that we are God's children, under God's providence, loved and called to a birth, life, meaning, and significance that is unique and infinitely precious. We sense too that we are precious not on the basis of what we accomplish or achieve during our lives, but simply on the basis of being created and loved by God.

But this intuition, however deeply felt, normally wilts under the pressure of trying to live a life that is unique and special in a world in which billions of others are also trying to do the same thing. Can billions be infinitely precious and utterly unique?

In the end mediocrity, anonymity and mortality overwhelm us. We begin to fear that we are not precious nor under divine providence. There is instead the sense that we are merely mediocre hacks, trying to make the world believe that we are something different. One among billions of others, clawing and scratching for a little uniqueness, meaning and immortality!

When we feel like this, we begin to believe that we are precious and unique only when we accomplish something which precisely sets us apart and ensures that we are remembered. For most of us the task of adult life is that of guaranteeing our own preciousness, lovableness, meaning, immortality and sanctity.

In the end we do not believe that we have these, independent of our own accomplishments. Hence we cannot, without bitter frustration, live ordinary lives of anonymity, hidden in Christ.

Few things torment us and are as destructive of our peace and happiness as is this problem: we have set ourselves the impossible, frustrating, task of assuring for ourselves something which only God can give us.

Because of this ordinary life does not seem enough for us, and we live as restless, competitive, driven persons, who are forced, precisely, to fabricate a lie to cover up the fact that we are mediocre.

Why is ordinary life not enough for us? Why does it always seem that our lives are small-town, small-time, too insignificant, not exciting enough? Why do we habitually feel mediocre, dissatisfied, unhappy at being like everyone else?

Why the propensity to leave our mark? Why is there such a torment in the insufficiency of everything attainable? Why does our own situation so often feel oppressively domestic?

Why, like Jonathan Livingston Seagull, do we want to fly above the rest, to leave the pack behind, and to somehow be more special than others? Why can we not embrace each other as sisters and brothers and, in humility and gratitude, rejoice in each other's gifts and each other's existence? Why the feeling that the other is a rival?

Why the need for masks, for pretense, for hype, for all kinds of lies that let us project certain images about ourselves?

Because we are trying to give ourselves something that only God can give us, ultimate uniqueness, significance and immortality.

Protestantism has always proclaimed that the central part of Christ's message is the statement: "Faith alone saves." We are justified by faith alone. They are right. That simple line reveals the final secret, namely that God gives eternal life. Preciousness, meaning, significance and immortality are free gifts from God.

If we could believe that, we would become a whole lot more restful, peaceful, humble, less competitive, grateful and happy. We would no longer hopelessly pursue the search for the holy grail. Ordinary life, in all its domesticity, shared with billions of others, would contain enough to ensure our preciousness, meaning, and significance.

Ordinary life is enough. Preciousness and significance come from being loved by God, not from what we can achieve. In the end we are not mediocre, and there is no need to fabricate the vital lie.

Curing Fire by Fire

IN HIS *Four Quartets* T. S. Eliot contrasts two kinds of fire:

> The only hope, or else despair
> Lies in the choice of pyre or pyre—
> To be redeemed from fire by fire.

What Eliot captures here is the deepest and most painful of all human choices, the alternative between God's flames and those of our own making. What is implied here?

We are born dis-eased, erotic, full of tension, relentlessly restless, full of fire. To be a human being is to be on fire for a consummation, a restfulness, a love, a symphony which, in this life, perpetually escapes us. In every cell of our bodies and in every area of our minds and hearts there is a fire, a restless ache, a burning for someone or something we have not yet experienced.

What comes naturally to us because of this is restless and compulsive activity. Being on fire, we are greedy for experience and find it hard ever to be satisfied or to come to rest. So much of what we do in life comes not from a free center inside us but from restlessness and compulsiveness. We are perpetually dissatisfied and unable to live within the spirit of our own lives. Our lives seem always to be too small, too petty, too domestic, too unimportant because we are on fire for bigger things, more important jobs, more important places.

Moreover this fire, this relentless restlessness, does not

necessarily suggest that somehow we are living wrongly. Its source is our own depth, the infinite caverns of our minds and hearts. Philosophers and anthropologists have always distinguished human from beast on the basis of rationality. In my own anthropology classes, I like to phrase that somewhat more humorously by stating that the difference between human and beast is that animals munch grass contentedly in meadows while humans smoke it discontentedly in bars . . . in there lies the difference! And that difference issues from different depths of mind and heart. Animals are not deep, humans are.

Given our infinite depth and our infinite hungers, in this life we will always be on fire. The fire inside us will never be extinguished by attaining the right experiences—the right partner in love, the right job, the right city, the right friends, the right recognition. Our choice is not between restlessness and restfulness, but between two kinds of restlessness, between two kinds of fire—"pyre and pyre."

We are destined to be consumed by one kind of fire or another, but the flames are very different—God's flames or those of our own choosing.

The solution to our restlessness, our fire, is to let it be consumed and transformed by a higher fire, a higher eros, a higher restlessness, the eros of God.

What is implied here? In a nutshell, what is meant is that we must widen our longings, deepen our aches, raise further still our psychic temperatures so that we burn precisely for the final consummation, the final symphony, God's kingdom.

Several years ago, after giving a conference on celibacy to a group of seminarians, I was approached by one of them with this complaint: "I am tired of abstract talk about sexuality. It's all useless because nobody can tell us what to actually do with sexual tension."

What can be done with unresolved tension, sexual or otherwise? We can pick it up, enter it, widen and deepen it, and let it be transformed by something still deeper, Christ's loneliness. Fire must be redeemed by fire, eros by Eros, aching by aching, frustration by advent, restless compulsion by gestation.

Great spiritual writers have always told us that we should imitate Christ not by trying to look as he looked, or even by trying to do the precise things that he did. Rather we should imitate Christ by trying to feel like he felt, by trying to imitate his motivation, that is, his deep longing for the consummation of everybody and everything in one community of love and peace.

That feeling is a fire, a restlessness, an ache, an eroticism. But it is a fire that does not lead to a compulsive greed for experience or to a restless incapacity to receive the spirit of one's own life. Rather it is a restlessness that leads one to genuinely live in advent, that is, to become pregnant with the gifts of the Holy Spirit—charity, joy, peace, patience, goodness, long-suffering, constancy, mildness and chastity—and gestate the conditions within which all fire and longing can be consumed by the fire and longing of God.

Who then devised the torment? Love.

2

THE UNFINISHED SYMPHONY: DREAMS AND FRIENDSHIP

What you dream alone remains a dream, what you dream with others can become reality.

(EDWARD SCHILLEBEECKX)

The Unfinished Symphony

STRANGE what meaning lies in paradox and anomaly!

In defeat there is a victory, in humiliation there is glory, in confusion there is always a new clarity, in the absurd one finds meaning, in tears lie relief, and in virtually every death there is new and deeper life.

Recently I wrote an article about a young woman making her perpetual commitment as a religious sister.

I stated both how much I admired her for the courage and vision to make such vows within a culture that rejects them and how much these vows themselves have a clarity and beauty precisely because they make the truth they express repellent and so drive all who witness them inward, forcing them to assimilate the truth in a new way.

I have been the recipient of some strange looks and questions since: Repellent vows? Really!

I am not without gratitude for this critique because it has forced me to clarify something I had just dimly felt but could not express, until now.

Now, with some help from an answer Thomas Merton once gave to an interviewer who asked him how he felt about celibacy, I want to spell out what is inchoately expressed in that term "repellent."

I will focus on just one of the vows, celibacy, because it is generally within that vow that one experiences this repellency in all its poignancy—and it is within that vow that the greatest danger for pathology lies. The principle involved in living that vow applies as well to poverty and obedience.

A celibate life is of itself an absurdity, pure and simple. Man without woman and woman without man is absurd.

"It is not good for the man to be alone!" When God spoke those words he meant them for everyone forever.

To be celibate is to live in incompleteness, unwholeness and inconsummation, in a loneliness that God himself has damned.

Further this is not merely a matter of celibates having or not having good interpersonal relations. A vision prevalent to-day contends that good heterosexual or homosexual friendships and a supportive community can and should offset the pain and unnaturalness of celibacy. After all, sexuality is more than just having sex and celibates need not be excluded from the realm of loving.

There is some truth in that, some wisdom, but also a lot of naïveté. Friendship and supportive community are critical, in the long run more important than sex.

But that fact does not offset the emotional crucifixion of celibacy because it cannot bypass the fact that however deep an unmarried friendship might be and however good and supportive community may be, within these, the members do not make a one, nor come to a consummation, in a way that satisfies the condition of Genesis: "that is why a man leaves his father and his mother and clings to his wife and the two become one flesh."

In a sexual relationship within a marriage a man and a woman make one, in a way that a man and a woman (or a woman and a woman or a man and a man) do not make in any unmarried friendship or community, however deep these latter relationships may be.

Hence outside married sexual relationship one will always live in a loneliness which has been condemned by the Creator himself.

However, I suspect, and I know from my married friends, that this loneliness exists too within marriage, even within the best of marriages.

Within a good marriage there are moments in which loneliness is transcended, but these moments are brief and usually point to a further, more difficult, place where, ultimately, two lonely and unconsummated, though married, persons elect to save one another from absurdity by being absurd together—for life. Hence what I write here applies as well to married persons.

At this point I suspect the tone of this article must sound masochistic. But this is not a masochistic answer.

It is in freely accepting this limit, this pathos, that we rise above ourselves and become more human, because it is then that we let go of those imaginings and unrealistic expectations which prevent us from living in advent for God's kingdom.

But this implies that we stop lying. The celibate condition, in the course of time, has become encrusted with pious lies, just as the married one has become encrusted with a false romanticism.

The lies and the romanticism serve to hide the real pain, the real tragedy, and the real meaning and nobility of both vocations because they hide the fact that in both celibacy and marriage the symphony remains unfinished.

A damned loneliness always exists. We remain painfully sexed, separate, partially always alone.

Only when this foolishness is recognized does inconsummation become thirst for a wider love, then self-pity turns into hope, confusion into clarity, foolishness into beauty.

Then absurdity becomes a center of peace and there, finally, things begin to make some sense and both marriage and celibacy become possible and beautiful.

Friendship Is Liberating Too

I WAS RAISED to believe that prayer and private morality were the foundations of the spiritual life. They were non-negotiable.

You were considered a good Christian if you prayed, privately and liturgically, and if your private morals were in order.

The Catholicism I was raised on, while never denying the importance of social justice, rarely impressed upon me the fact that involvement with the struggle of the poor was just as nonnegotiable as prayer and private morality.

The conscience of Christianity has changed. Perhaps the most critical development within all Christianity these past years has not been the changes brought in by Vatican II but the reemergence of the idea that there can be no spiritual health without social justice.

Liberation theologians from the Third World and social justice advocates within our own culture have helped irrevocably re-impress into the Christian conscience the idea that social justice is nonnegotiable, that it is not an extra we can choose to get involved in or not, just as prayer and private morality are not optional.

To be a healthy Christian means *to pray, to live a good moral life, and to be involved with the poor.* All three of these are nonnegotiable.

But this is not so easily conceded by all, as recent tensions within the church show.

Social justice movements are often accused of not empha-
sizing sufficiently private conversion, private prayer and private morality. The criticism is made that they are producing
a spirituality with an underdeveloped private conscience—
that is, it does not matter whether you pray, hold grudges,
are one-sided, live sexually beyond the seventh commandment, or attend church or not, as long as you work for the
right causes.

Conversely, on their part, they make the criticism that,
for the most part, Christianity has dangerously privatized
conversion and produced a spirituality with an underdeveloped social conscience—namely, you are a good Christian as
long as you say your prayers and attend church and obey the
church's sexual commandments, irrespective of whether you
are ignoring or even positively exploiting the poor.

There is some truth and some exaggeration in the accusations of both sides, though at this time, because of an imbalance in the direction of private conversion, I submit, the
church must be more sensitive to the criticism made by the
proponents of social justice.

Their criticism, save for a few exaggerated expressions, is
correct and biting:

Why is it that a Christian may not, in good conscience, ignore the teachings of Scripture and the church regarding prayer
and private morality, and yet she or he may, in good conscience, ignore the social teachings of Scripture and the church?

Thus, for example, the church's teachings which have to
do with sexual ethics (e.g. *Humanae Vitae*) tend to be seen as
the deciding criteria determining who is good or bad as a
Christian, while the church's teaching on social issues (for
example *Mater et Magistra*), which have equal moral and
dogmatic authority, can be largely ignored in good conscience.

That's an imbalance in need of correction. But there is still a further imbalance:

Through much pain, we have come to realize that prayer alone is not enough, social justice is also needed. Now, through more pain, we are coming to realize that prayer and social justice, together but alone, are also not enough. Why do I say this? Because too many persons who both pray and do social justice are angry, bitter, lacking in gratitude and joy, and full of hate. What is lacking? In a word, friendship.

A healthy spiritual life is anchored on three pillars, *prayer, social justice* and *friendship*. The latter is as critical and nonnegotiable as the former. Without the warming and mellowing that good friendship brings into life, we invariably lose gratitude and joy.

To pray and to do social justice is to be prophetic. But that's a lonely and hard business. Prophets are persecuted, are powerless and are rejected. Because of this, it is all too easy to get angry, to feel self-righteous, to fill with bitterness, to become selective in our prophecy and to hate the very people we are trying to save.

When this happens, gratitude and joy disappear from our lives and we are unable to live without the need to be angry. Invariably, then, both our prayer and social action become perverse.

We become recognized not for our joy and love, but for our anger and bitterness. Our prophetic words are spoken not out of love and grief, but out of indignation. We turn poverty into an ideology by losing sight of the end of the struggle—namely, celebration, joy, play, embrace, forgiveness.

Only friendship can save us. Loving, challenging friends who can melt our bitterness and free us from the need to be angry are as critical within the spiritual life as are prayer and social justice. To neglect friendship is to court bitterness and perversion.

There are three key questions to ask ourselves when we are evaluating spiritual health:

1. Do I pray every day?
2. Am I involved with the struggle of the poor?
3. Do I have the kinds of friendships in my life which move me beyond bitterness and anger?

Women, Men and Friendship

THE GERMAN POET Rainer Maria Rilke once wrote: "Perhaps the sexes are more similar than we think . . . and thus the great renewal of our world consists in this: that man and maid, freed from all false feeling and aversion, might come together as friends, as neighbours, as more than lovers—as brothers and sisters."

One of the deep wounds in Western culture is that men and women find it very hard to be friends. It's easy for them to be lovers, but not friends.

I don't know how often I have had people of both sexes complain to me about the difficulty of finding friendship with the opposite sex. Invariably the comment is: "It is so much easier to find a lover than a friend." That is normally, too, spoken with a touch of sadness.

Good, healthy, open, chaste, life-giving heterosexual friendship is rare. It is not that we do not crave for it or value it, it is just that we rarely find it.

Why?

At one level the answer is easy. Sexual tension takes away easefulness. Consciously and unconsciously, every deep heterosexual friendship is partly manipulated by sexual tension. We need not be unduly apologetic about this.

In heterosexual friendships there will be tensions, hesitations, awkwardness, inhibitions and hidden agendas. Sex is too powerful to allow men and women to be easily honest and upfront in friendship.

Everything is sexually charged and so nearly every action can be taken to imply something else and, consequently, there is a lot of cautiousness in our reaching out to each other.

That caution is often well-founded. We should not be naïve about the power of sexuality. There is a natural dynamism within sexuality that pushes toward genitality. Deep relationships between men and women, by nature, cry out for sexual consummation. That is deep within instinct and written into the very way God made us.

This makes our coming together as friends very difficult.

But there are other reasons for this difficulty beyond the natural incurable push of sexuality itself. To the natural disease of sexuality, our culture adds a pansexuality and an obsession with genitality. Today virtually everything has a sexual innuendo, and having sex is, more or less, an extension of dating.

In such a setting, our understanding of love, sex, and friendship narrows. The Greeks saw six aspects to love: eros, sexual attraction, falling in love; ludus, playfulness, love as a game; philia, friendship, care; mania, obsessional love, infatuation, dark eros; pragma, sensible, committed love; and agape, selfless, altruistic love.

Our culture tends to define love basically in terms of eros and mania. To love someone is to be romantically obsessed with them and to want sex with them.

When this is true, then sexuality quickly becomes just sex. It is no longer understood, first and foremost, as a dimension of self-awareness, as a hunger of the soul for wholeness, community, family, creativity, friendship, affection and play.

In our culture's view, a view we have generally interiorized and made our own, to love means to make love, to be a lover.

Platonic heterosexual friendship is seen as too incomplete, too empty, or as simply unrealistic. No wonder men and women find it hard to be in deep friendship with each other!

When to love someone means to make love to that someone, then it becomes hard to trust that simple friendship might be more life-giving than having sex.

I find that, in our culture, most people have given up on the ideal of deep life-giving friendships between women and men. This despair usually expresses itself, not in a knife to the wrist or in a downed bottle of pills, but in the kind of statement that the young man makes to Cher in the movie *Moonstruck*: "I know this is all wrong! We probably don't love each other and are all wrong for each other and we are going to mess up our lives and our families, but come up to my room this instant and let's go to bed!"

Few things are as healing and life-giving as is friendship between woman and man, man and woman. As God said, "it is not good for the man to be alone!"

With Rilke, I believe that, in the end, friendship survives longer than sex and spawns a wider, deeper, more life-giving intimacy.

But it is rare. Deep, intimate, chaste heterosexual friendship is no small achievement. We lack for models and are virtual pioneers in this partially uncharted area.

Heterosexual friendships require a delicate balance between caution and risk, between inhibition and daring vulnerability. But they are worth the risk and the effort.

When we write our autobiographies, hopefully, like Anne Dillard, we can write something like this: "I would give my heart to one oddball after another . . . and for years on end, and forsook everything else in life, and rightly so, to begin learning with them that unplumbed intimacy that is life's chief joy." (*An American Childhood*)

Emerging from Stone

A POWERFUL and haunting piece of sculpture by Michelangelo is entitled *The Awakening Slave*. It shows a body struggling to emerge from stone, to pull itself free. Part of the body is already clearly formed, the rest is still inchoate, hidden and imprisoned in stone.

Few images capture as much the feeling of what it means to be human! Born as infants we are helpless, with little self-consciousness, dependent, unable to speak, unable to really know ourselves and others, bound by countless limitations.

In the moment of birth we partly emerge from the stone. The rest of our life is a struggle to be born further, to pull ourselves further free.

But, very early, we sense that it is hard. We are so limited in our intelligence, in our energy, in our psyches, in our emotions, in our moral abilities, in our relationships and in our physical make-up.

We push too hard and something breaks! There is only one place where we do not sense our limits, only one place where we can fly, free of stone—in our dreams. In the kind that we dream in our ideals (not the kind we dream at night) we can truly dance, fly, love perfectly, be totally beyond our own and others' limits.

There are no limitations of energy, love, relationships or emotion in our dreams. There we can pull ourselves completely free from the stone and, then, turn around and look at our actual imprisonment.

Unfortunately too many of us no longer dream. Dreaming is out of fashion. Realism, cynicism and despair are in vogue. To dream today is to be laughed at, ridiculed, to be regarded as naïve, childish and, ultimately, as pitiable.

We see this, for example, in the common reaction to anything that is idealistic, romantic, virginal or contains the type of things we used to write poetry about.

Nobody seems to be challenged by these things any more to dream dreams, to push themselves into deeper and more special realms. Mostly these things are met with cynicism and disbelief, coupled with the urge to debunk and with the pitying condescension that we save for the especially naïve. Kid's stuff!

I am saddened by this critique. I have seen hopelessness, the lack of dreams, in eighty-year-olds in bad health, shunted off unwanted, to die in auxiliary homes because nobody wants them any longer. It is justifiably hard for them to dream!

But when I see, basically, the same hopelessness in gifted, beautiful, richly endowed young people with every practical reason in the world to be dreaming great dreams, I can only be saddened. Despair—and so young. Why?

We have stopped dreaming. We have got sucked in by an unvirginal cynicism of an age which confuses despair with realism. We have stopped struggling and, bottom line, we have despaired that we can ever have a profound relationship, a real romance, genuine community, aesthetic love or full sexuality.

Belief in them is like belief in Santa Claus and the Easter Bunny. That's for kids! We have settled for what we can have, second best, and are cynical about any more idealistic realities.

Those of us who are married are no longer trying to attain the optimum with our partner. We have settled for some less demanding second best, or are looking elsewhere.

Those of us who are celibate are no longer trying, with all the incredible tension this involves, to love genuinely yet celibately. Our cynicism has declared that the ideal is impossible and so we become either a sterile old bachelor or maid, or we live a double standard.

All cynicism is despair, pure and simple. All refusal to dream dreams of something beyond is a giving up, a resignation to mediocrity, a self-imposed condemnation to remain partly unborn, in prison. Despair is simply the defeat of our dreams of greatness.

Few things mire us as deeply in the stone as does our refusal to believe in the ideal. "There is only one real sin," Doris Lessing once remarked, "and that is calling second best by anything other than what it really is, second best!"

Moreover it is important that we do not just dream alone. Dreams need to be shared. What we dream alone remains a dream, what we dream with others becomes a reality! Pain and imprisonment result because people have no one to dream with. No person can cut themselves free of the stone by themselves. We achieve nothing truly in isolation.

We need to dream and to share those dreams: build dream castles in our minds, ideal loves and communities in our hearts. We cannot get fully out of the stone in fact, but we can in desire, in our dreams.

They are the chisel which we can use to slowly cut away the stone and enable ourselves to emerge to further birth. Everything can be overcome if we dream. Through dreams we see the end of our exile.

Does all this sound like the ravings of an unrealistic

dreamer? The naïve daydreams and the wishful thinking of a young man out of touch with reality? The rantings of someone with delusions of grandeur?

Perhaps! They are the dreams of a young man, a very idealistic one in fact. And, yes, he has delusions of grandeur! But they are not my dreams. You can read about them in John's Gospel, chapter 17.

Dare to Be One in a Thousand

RECENTLY I was giving a talk to a group of young adults preparing for marriage and was trying to challenge them with the Christian teaching on love and sexuality. They were objecting constantly.

When I had finished speaking a young man stood up and said, "Father, I agree with your principles, in the ideal. But you are totally unrealistic. Do you know what is going on out here? Nobody is living that stuff anymore. You'd have to be one person in a thousand to live what you're suggesting. Everyone is living differently now."

I looked at him, sitting beside a young woman whom he obviously loved deeply and hoped to marry, and decided to appeal to his idealism. I asked him, "When you marry that lady beside you, what kind of marriage do you want, one like everyone else's, or one in a thousand?"

"One in a thousand," he answered without hesitation.

"Then," I suggested, "you'd best do what only one in a thousand does. If you do what everyone else does, you will have a marriage like everyone else. If you do what only one in a thousand does, you can have a one-in-a-thousand marriage."

That is not complex theology, it is simple mathematics, but it needs to be said. More and more, as I lecture and write, I am being challenged by people, young and old, who are protesting against idealism. This protest takes many forms. Most commonly it sounds something like this: "Whether certain principles and values are true or false is not so relevant. What is relevant is that virtually everyone has decided to ignore them and live in a different way. Nobody is living like that anymore—everyone is living in this way now!"

Implicit in this is that if everyone is living in a certain way, then this way must be right. Values by common denominator. Principles by Gallup poll.

Occasionally this critique takes a more cynical bent: "Idealism is naïve, for kids. The mature, the realistic, do not live with their heads in the clouds. Hence, adjust, update, recognize what is there and accept it; live like everyone else is living."

What an incredible and tragic loss of idealism! Such a philosophy voices despair because the deepest demand of love, Christianity, and of life itself is precisely the challenge to specialness, to what is most ideal. Love, Christianity and life demand that we take the road less taken, that we be in restless cogitation for a higher eros, that we be one in a thousand.

Our culture, on the other hand, is rejecting this and is swallowing us whole. The current culture is reversing Robert Frost's famous adage and telling us "to take the road more taken." Prophecy is seen as unrealistic, idealism as immature. We are growing ever more dumb.

Hence our task today is to be leaven, to be idealistic and in that way to be prophetic.

Our culture's demand that everyone be like everyone else is not so much malicious as it is despairing. The death of idealism is a child of despair, always. People are content to settle for an attainable second-best only when, for whatever reasons (hurt, bad self-image, lack of hope), they have given up on ever attaining what is ultimately best.

Today we need prophets. We need people who, when speaking of love, economics, values, sexuality and aesthetics, are compassionate enough to be empathetic to our real struggles.

In being prophetic in this way, we can show the world that we truly love it because, ultimately, nobody wants a homogenized culture, nobody wants the lowest common denominator within relationships, love and sexuality, nobody wants to despair that we can feed the hungry and create a more just world, and nobody wants a world which despairingly says: "The best, what's truly special, cannot be reached, so simply settle for what is happening. Do what everyone else is doing, that's good enough!"

It is not good enough. What is truer and deeper inside us knows that there is more and wants more.

Philosophies, theologies and spiritualities which proclaim "do what everyone else is doing and that is good enough" break the sixth commandment, which says "Thou shalt not kill!"

John Paul II, in an address in West Germany in 1980, called on Christians to be prophets in this sense.

Our culture, he stated, tends to declare "human weakness a fundamental principle, and so make it a human right. Christ, on the other hand, taught that a person has above all a right to his or her own greatness."

Thirteen-year-old Anne Frank concurred:

That is the difficulty in these times: Ideals, dreams and cherished hopes rise within us, only to meet the horrible truth and be shattered. It's really a wonder that I haven't dropped my ideals, because they seem so absurd and impossible to carry out. Yet I must uphold my ideals, for perhaps the time will come when I will be able to carry them out. (July 15th, 1944, third from last entry in her diary)

May we have the courage to uphold our ideals, even when we cannot fully live them.

Remembering as Surgery

THERE IS A FINE LINE between nostalgia and the longing for lost innocence. The latter is healthy, the former is not.

Nostalgia is an unhealthy depression, an adolescent sentimentality which leaves us clinging to the past so as to be unable to enter the present with verve and vitality. In the end it is a mummification, an unnatural embalming of something which is dead.

For a Christian there is the challenge to move beyond that, to let go, to not cling, to accept death, loss and corruption in order to be open to accept the new life and new spirit that the present brings.

Unfortunately nostalgia comes upon us looking like the angel of light, with a power to touch our deepest parts in the same way as we are touched by real love and truth.

But in the final analysis, like masturbation, it never deals with something which touches depth. Of itself it is a turning away from reality in favor of fantasy. Not surprisingly it carries with it the appropriate concomitant depression. These words are harsh, but they need to stand as a preamble for what follows.

We all need, occasionally, to make a recessive journey to our origins, to our youth, our innocence, to that place in time and in our hearts, before our sophistication, when we were truly young, simple and happy. Such a journey refocuses us and gives us a renewed sense of what is truest in us.

But such a journey is not a sentimental voyage into the

past in which we recall our youth, its simplicity and its innocence, and then bring appropriate lessons and guilts to bear
upon the present. That would only lead to depression.

The recessive journey, rather, is not so much a re-
examination of our past as it is an examination of what is
truest in us. In the deepest part of our hearts lie our real
roots. At the end of that journey we find that our life has not
been lost, blown, screwed up beyond hope or irrevocably
wounded into melancholy by death, sin and loss.

The journey to remember, to recall origins, is not a sentimentality, it is a surgery, a cutting away of cancerous overlay
to set the heart, in its primal and perennial vitality and innocence, free.

I made some such journeys lately. I did some remembering. Partly it was nostalgia, partly surgery.

The recall of myself as a child is both humbling and humiliating; more the former. We were poor and many around
an old wooden table in that immigrant district of rural
Saskatchewan. On a farm too small we struggled to learn a
new language, to become educated, to do more than just
make do, but for years we struggled just to survive.

I am younger than the depression, but I can recall the
winter of 1955. We were so poor then. We were always poor.

My overriding memory of childhood is that of being hungry, not so much for food, but more for a world beyond that
of economic and social poverty, for a world beyond a small
isolated farm, for a life and an experience beyond a world in
which there was no hot water on tap and in which there was
not even the capability of speaking the language properly or
dressing properly.

I felt cursed then by the sense that I was poor. And I was,
in some ways, moving in my patched, hand-me-down clothes,

too often smelling of farmyard and barnyard. The shame of poverty hits hardest in the teen years.

To step back into that now can still bring flushes of humiliation. To truly recall it, however, brings a healthy humbling coupled with a strength and a sense of richness that nourishes like Elijah's jug.

We were rich in fact, all of us growing up in poverty on those immigrant farms. Our houses and hearts contained all that is important.

Dirty, barefoot, speaking in our multiple accents, we were full of excitement. Our hearts were keen, clear as crystal, eager to learn and full of appreciation. There was enough love and innocence around.

My life has been blessed with various kinds of riches and successes since then. Through travel, lecturing, teaching and friendships I have been given the opportunity to experience in reality most of what I dreamed about as a runny-nosed, but wide eyed, child.

But with the success and experience has come a crippling pseudo-sophistication, an unfreedom, a lack of innocence, a certain fatigue of the spirit, and a fear that can make a recessive journey to my origins an event of depressive nostalgia. The verve, the happiness, the innocence, why are they too often lacking?

Lately I have had to take to dreaming again.

It is time, when that happens, to take a recessive journey, to go back to the farm, to recall one's origins. In remembering there is a surgery. When we were little boys and girls our hearts were so eager to learn, our spirits so hungry and welcoming. So much was gift.

Lord, let it all be gift again!

Single Life Offers Opportunities

The refusal of woman is a fault in my chastity . . . and all my compensations are a desperate and useless expedient to cover this irreparable loss which I have not fully accepted.

I can learn to accept it in the spirit and in love and it will no longer be "irreparable." The cross repairs and transforms it. The tragic chastity which suddenly realizes itself to be mere loss, and the fear that death has won—that one is sterile, useless, hateful. I do not say this is my lot, but in my vow I can see this as an ever-present possibility. (Quoted in J. H. Griffin, *Follow the Ecstasy*)

THOSE ARE THE WORDS of Thomas Merton as he reflects upon the dangers of not marrying.

In sexual inconsummation, be it a deliberately chosen state or one imposed by circumstance, there is always the feeling, seldom far from the surface, that there is something sterile within one's existence.

Merton designated this as "a fault in one's chastity," a fault which can either be tragic or transformed by the cross.

I have thought about this a lot, not just as it pertains to my own celibate existence, but especially as it pertains to persons living a single life in the world.

For many of them life can seem particularly unfair. Society is set up for couples. They are alone. Society has accepted and made a place for consecrated religious. However singles in the world, while sharing the celibate lot of consecrated religious, share virtually none of their security or advantages.

Moreover, unlike married persons and consecrated religious, singles in the world are rarely given a thriving set of symbols which can provide a symbolic hedge within which to understand their inconsummation. Too often single persons in the world feel they are looking in at life from the outside, that they are abnormal, that they are missing fundamentally something within life.

Consequently, unlike married persons and consecrated religious, few single persons feel they have positively chosen their state of life. They feel victimized into it. Few single persons feel relaxed, easeful and accepting of their lot.

The feeling instead is always that this must be temporary. Rarely can a young single person project his or her future acceptingly to the end and see him- or herself growing old and dying single and happy. Invariably the feeling is this: Something has to happen to change this! I do not choose this! I cannot see myself for the rest of my life like this!

There are immense dangers in these feelings. First there is the danger of simply never fully and joyfully picking up one's life and seeing it as worthwhile, of never choosing to be what one is, of never accepting the spirit that fits the life that one is actually living.

As well, there is the danger of panicking and marrying simply because marriage is seen as a panacea and no possibility of real happiness is seen outside it.

Some of these feelings are good. The truth sets us free and so it is not good to pretend. Pious lies, denial, or spiritualities of espousal with God which do little to placate the emotions, cannot erase the facts: "It is not good for the man to be alone," the universe works in pairs, the absence of consummation creates a fault in one's chastity which the Creator himself has condemned.

To be single is to be different, more different than we often dare admit.

But it is in the admitting that truth can set us free. However, for that to happen, certain things must be understood and accepted.

Sexuality is a dimension of our self-awareness. We awake to consciousness and feel ourselves, at every level, as cut off, sexed, lonely monads separated and aching for unity.

Celibacy is a fault in our chastity.

However, to be single is not necessarily to be asexual or sterile. Today sometimes the impression is given that sexual union is happiness and no happiness is possible outside that. That is a superficial and dangerous algebra.

Sexuality is the drive in us toward connection, community, family, friendship, affection, love, creativity and generativity. We are happy and whole when these things are in our lives, not on the basis of whether or not we sleep alone.

The single celibate life offers its own unique opportunities for achieving these. God never closes one door without opening a few others.

In recognizing that it is easier to find a lover than a friend, we also recognize that human sexuality and generativity are more than biological.

Biology is one thing, but there are other ways of being deeply sexual, other ways of getting pregnant and impregnating, other kinds of sexual intimacy and other ways of being mother and father.

There is a mysterious dynamic within separation and community. Sexuality and community function at various levels.

I remember a young man I worked with several years

back. He was discerning between religious life and marriage. At one point he commented:

"I have always been afraid of being a priest because it will mean dying alone. My father died when I was fifteen and he died in my mother's arms. I have always rejected the celibate state because I want to die like my father died—in a woman's arms.

"However one day I was meditating on Christ's life and it struck me powerfully that he died alone, loved, but in nobody's arms. He was really alone, though he was powerfully linked to everyone in a different way. It struck me that this could also be a good way to die!"

3

PASSION, LOVE AND SEX

To love a person is to say, you at least will
not die!

(Gabriel Marcel)

Romance Gives an Inkling of Heaven

A CANADIAN POET, J. S. Porter, has published a book of poems under the title *The Thomas Merton Poems* (Moonstone Press, 1988). His claim is that Merton might have written these poems had he lived longer. Merton, I suspect, would indeed recognize himself in them.

One poem which particularly caught my eye is without title:

> There's too much of everything
>   books, stars, flowers.
> How can one flower be precious
>   in a bed of thousands?
> How can a book count
>   in a library of millions?
> The universe is a junkyard
>   burnt out meteors, busted up stars
>   planetary cast offs, throwaway galaxies
>   born and buried in an instant
>   repeating, repeating
> Yet something remains
>   the dream of fewness
>   one woman, one man.

There was a time in my life when this poem would have burned holes into me and left me haunted and restless. The dream of fewness/one woman, one man.

It still touches the deepest parts of me and triggers a certain ache; but there are now other parts of me that raise questions that were not until recently inside me.

Is this dream a dream of the adolescent? Are we longing for a teenage crush? Is it speaking of something more aptly termed obsessional neurosis? Does it refer to something we are meant to outgrow, first fervor, untransformed love? Are we talking here of naïve, unrealistic Hollywood daydreams? Are we talking here of a narcissistic longing to find another lonely person with whom to gang-up against genuine community? Are we talking here about a dream of a sick privatized, selfish love which (as Marxism suggested years ago) hinders the movement toward justice and wider community? Is this a dream for dizzy romance or for what's most precious in God's kingdom?

These questions themselves need questioning. What is their root? Are they the fruit of growing up or are they the fruit of cynicism, tiredness, a fatigued spirit, and a heart that has lost its ideals and is content with second best?

I suspect it is some of both. The dream of fewness can be adolescent and can lead to much useless restlessness and aching. Its pursuit can be counterproductive of community and a hindrance to justice. However the loss of this dream can also indicate a heart that has lost its most important fire for life and has domesticated its passion.

The dream of fewness comes from our wildest longings and is an ache for a great love. As such, whatever its dysfunctions, it is God's lure pulling us toward our real aim, glory.

Nobody who still believes in the dream of fewness needs the reminder that we "do not live by bread alone," that there is infinitely more to living than the simple sweetening of life. This dream spawns within us a deep and unrelenting restlessness which, perhaps more than anything else, can push us beyond our instinct to settle in, consume, hoard, be secure and let the amusements and distractions of the good life be somehow enough for us.

To dream the dream of fewness is to know, right within the restless stirring of one's own heart, that one is, as both Scripture and philosophy affirm, fired into life with a madness that comes from the gods and which demands that one attain a great love.

It is only when we despair of attaining that great love that we grow embarrassed with romance, with "falling in love," with the dream of fewness and attempt to tame our longings by subduing them with phrases like naïve, adolescent, counterproductive of community, sickly privatized, and obsessional neurosis.

Already a generation ago C. S. Lewis commented upon this:

> In speaking of this desire . . . I feel a certain shyness. I am almost committing an indecency. I am trying to rip open the inconsolable secret in each one of you—the secret which hurts so much that you take revenge on it by calling it names like nostalgia and romanticism and adolescence, the secret also which pierces with such sweetness that, when, in very intimate conversation, the mention of it becomes imminent, we grow awkward and affect to laugh at ourselves, the secret we cannot hide and cannot tell.

A friend of mine who was getting married tried to assure me that she knew what she was getting into: "I'm being realistic, Father, this isn't naïve passion. I'm not looking for Hollywood romance."

I sent her the poem on the dream of fewness with a note

that read something like this: "Enjoy the first fruits of your love, your honeymoon, the dream of fewness. It's one of the better foretastes of heaven given us in this life. The accidents of life, soon enough, deprive us of that. Taste and remember!"

The dream of fewness. Taste and remember. Think of how much happier and mellower and centered beyond the immediate the world would be if everyone had tasted and could remember.

Passion Is God's Fire in Us

FIFTY YEARS AGO T. S. Eliot predicted the death of passion, poetry, fidelity and historical consciousness. Today, tragically, that prediction is coming true.

As Christians we need to recognize that fact and respond, in order to defend passion and challenge people to it.

That sounds strange and it is. Passion has, at least so it seems, always been distrusted in religious circles and extolled in secular ones. Indeed the secular world tended to claim passion as its own, as something irreligious, as the very force which is rebellious against religion and which, if responded to, frees one from the shackles of religion.

Preachers, priests, spiritual writers and church leaders tended to help this idea along. The church, it seemed, was forever lashing out against passion, pointing out its dangers and forbidding people to allow themselves to feel and enjoy the full emotional, psychological and instinctual force of their eros.

Passion was made to seem at odds with religion.

How wrong we were! And how wrong the secular world has discovered itself to be! There has been a strange and ironic reversal.

Today the secular world is trying to rid itself of all passion and the church is suddenly, much to its own surprise, finding itself in the novel position of having to defend passion. Why this turn of events?

Because the secular world has discovered passion to be a

very inconvenient thing. Passion, romance, poetry, aesthetics, all these things, challenge infidelity.

Thus our culture has begun to classify passion as it classifies other religious things, namely as something medieval, the product of naïveté, as something from which people need to be freed.

How deliciously ironic! The very force that it had so long claimed as uniquely its own, trumpeted as its victory, has, when given rein, proved to be an inconvenient embarrassment. Passion, in the end, is only for religious persons. Why?

Because our world exalts a false kind of freedom. In our society today we are exhorted to hang loose, to run from involvement, to run away from anything that might tie us down. We are invited to live as "free spirits," soaring, fulfilled, unencumbered.

Passion and romance spell death for that kind of freedom. Passion means involvement, attachment, surrender, a loss of control and freedom, commitment. If sustained, it means fidelity.

For this reason it is no accident that, for the most part, secular wisdom today considers passion in the same way as it considers religion—kid's stuff, for the naïve.

Today passion and romance are seen as things we need therapy from. In his astute and very disturbing book, *The Triumph of the Therapeutic*, Philip Rieff, who is no friend of religion, points out that in our present culture passion and romance are "archaic and dispensable." They are what Freud calls "erotic illusions" and, as Rieff goes on to say, it is time we stopped organizing our personalities and our communities around them.

Love and hatred, the products of passion, are, in his words, obsolete as organizing modes of personality. In a culture of contacts and infidelity, passion and romance are experienced as tyranny.

Bottom line, today romantic love is considered a neurosis, a sickness or, at best, something for the very young or very naïve, a hangover from former ages, as is religion.

For this reason it is important that Christians and the Christian churches rush to the defense of passion and romance. They are part of God's fire in us, a great gift, to be channeled prudently, it is true, but none the less to be ever perceived precisely as a gift from God.

Today they are badly needed. They challenge infidelity.

When T. S. Eliot predicted the death of poetry, passion, fidelity and historical consciousness, it is no accident that he placed all of these together. They flow from each other. Passion and poetry, when released and given, bond us to each other and to history in a way that makes infidelity and false freedom much more difficult.

In a culture characterized by flightiness, lack of commitment, hanging loose, infidelity, cynicism and programmed boredom, we need fire, passion and romance.

They perhaps more than anything else can help turn the tide and become the vaccine which immunizes us against the infectious bacteria set loose by the cynicism and infidelity of our age.

The fire of passion comes from God. Eros is at the root of human soul and body. In the Hasidic tradition there is a famous parable about a man who wanted to be a blacksmith. So he bought a hammer, an anvil and bellows. But he could not bend any iron. There was no flame, no heat in his forge. He had everything except the thing he most needed—the spark, the fire, the heat that makes things malleable.

In a world in which fidelity and historical consciousness

are dying and being replaced by infidelity and programmed boredom, in a world in which true romance and true sexuality are being replaced by schizophrenic sex and pornography, we need fire in the forge, passion and romance.

Christians need to arise in the defense of eros.

Love Is Coming Home

THE HUMAN HEART is complex. Many of us have learned this through much pain.

It can give us the assurance that what we are experiencing is truly love and then, itself, abandon the very feeling that it led us to believe was love.

Most of us, I suspect, have had the experience of making a mistake in love—of mistaking infatuation for love, or having love go sour, or of having one love wilt before another infatuation.

Too late, we realize that the feeling we felt would last forever simply changed or disappeared and we were left with a sense of bitterness, disillusionment, and betrayal.

Given that, and given the human tragedies we call divorce, broken friendship and love gone sour, it is not surprising that there is a certain pain surrounding the question: How do I know what real love is?

How do I know whether my heart is playing tricks on me?

How do I know whether this person will make a good marriage partner, or friend, for me? How do I know whether I am just infatuated, or naïve, or even using someone?

There is no simple way to answer those questions since love is always partly mystery, partly blind, and partly inexplicable. However it is not totally blind and our responsibility toward others and ourselves requires that we try to discern real love from that which is more ephemeral.

What is real love? Real love is what we experience when we have the sense that we are coming home. Let me try to explain.

Robert Frost has commented that home is a place where they have to take you, it is not a place you have to earn or deserve. Henri Nouwen, speaking about his experience of living with handicapped adults in L'Arche, remarked: "What is so unique about living in L'Arche is that here I am loved by people who are in no way impressed with me."

What is contained in these comments can be very helpful in answering the question: How do I know what real love is?

Real love is always a coming home, it is not a place we deserve or earn, it is coming to a place where you sense others will love you without necessarily being impressed with you.

Thus real love is always experienced as a security, a safe place, home, a safe harbor which we sail into. It is a place of rest. For this reason it is experienced as a place from which you do not want to, or need to, go home.

Conversely infatuation and other kinds of bonding that can feel like real love are places of insecurity, of deep restlessness, places which "don't have to take us," which we have to earn, places where we have to perform and impress and from which, ultimately, we go home.

It is interesting how, in love and friendship, we can be infatuated and obsessively drawn to someone who is very different from ourselves—into whose heart we can never sail as into a safe harbor. It can be exciting and titillating being with that person. Perhaps, as in cases of infatuation, we might even need obsessively to be with that person, like a drug addict needs a fix.

But in the end, in spite of the excitement and obsession,

after we have had our fix we need to, and want to, go home. That person's heart can never, ultimately, be home for us.

Real love and real friendship are home—you do not go home from them! Whenever we experience love, however powerful, from which we need to go home, that love can be valuable and good in our lives, but it can never be a love upon which we can build a marriage or a truly intimate friendship.

Hence the criterion when choosing someone for marriage, or even just for intimate friendship, is the sense of coming home. Love is home.

Ultimately, if we cannot really be of one heart and mind with someone, however interesting and exciting that person may be, then that other will become just part of our world and we will grow apart and go our separate ways, that is, to our separate homes.

Given the complexities of the human heart, we can be obsessed with someone, painfully and hopelessly, and yet in that relationship not be at our right place in the universe. In the end our completeness, real love, home, lies elsewhere.

But the heart needs to be scrutinized carefully before it will tell us that. It has, as Pascal said, its reasons.

Yet at a certain level it rings true and will tell us where our true rest lies, namely at that place where we do not have to impress or perform, or earn or win, where we feel safe and secure and where we are at home.

Expressing Our Affection

CERTAIN QUESTIONS bring us pain. The question of love is frequently one of them.

Have you ever experienced a love that gave you the sense that you were lovable despite everything that is weak and lacking in you? Have you ever been loved unconditionally?

Oft-times these questions make us ache. We look at our lives and see a searing lack of unconditional love. The impression is that nobody loves us in a way that assures us at our deepest levels that we are lovable.

Our friendships, our loves, our families, our marriages appear to be anything but matrixes of unconditional love. At least so it seems.

But there is a confusion here. When we think of love, we think of affection. These are not always the same thing.

One kind of love is generally expressed through affection, through positive stroking, physical caressing, emotional affirmation and sexual intimacy.

But our experience of these is usually weak, only rarely is there enough physical touch, emotional stroking, expressed affection or satisfying sexual expression in our lives. Because of this, most times we feel unloved and perhaps even unlovable.

But these gestures of love are not identical with love.

Sometimes in our friendships, marriages, families and communities, there is beneath the lack of physical and emotional stroking, beneath the sexual frustrations, and beneath the harsh and angry words which are frequently exchanged, an unconditional concern and commitment. There is unconditional love. Unfortunately, because the love is not expressed in affection, that love remains largely unperceived.

When that happens then we do not *feel* that we are loved and there are negative consequences for our self-image. One part of us—the physical, emotional, sexual and affective part of us—begins to lose confidence and progressively atrophies.

We begin to feel that nobody loves us and to identify love entirely with what we are lacking, namely with physical, emotional, sexual and affective stroking.

I dealt with a middle-aged lady who felt like this. She had grown up in a family in which care and stability abounded but physical affection was never expressed. She had remained single and, save for a few dissatisfying sexual encounters which had been entered into because of depression and desperation, had never expressed physical affection in her life. Now she was convinced she had never been loved. When she thought of love she filled with pain, aching and bitterness.

Yet when she was able to move beyond the hurt and look at her life objectively she saw some things which surprised her. She had always been loved, solidly, deeply, unconditionally. She was also very lovable. Her strict Irish family had never been able to tell her through words, physical touch or emotional stroking that they loved her. But they had in fact loved her despite being affectively inarticulate. Their love had expressed itself in commitment, generosity, concern and fidelity.

But these were given too starkly, without affection being expressed, and this experience had remained constant throughout the rest of her life. In her friendships and relationships invariably the same pattern resurfaced.

She had indeed been loved for more than fifty years but, at one level of her being, had not known it. At another level she had known it. While she protested that she had a weak self-image and felt unlovable, she radiated stability and confidence and lovableness at every level of her being save the physical and sexual one. There she felt insecurity and lacked confidence.

Her story is a paradigm for all of us, God's poor, the little ones who go through life too starved for affection, convinced that we are not loved nor lovable, burdened with a bad self-image. We think we are not loved, but beneath it all we are strongly loved and lovable and possess a tremendous confidence and stability because of it.

Equally tragic is the reverse: many persons have a lot of physical, emotional and sexual affection in their lives yet, underneath, they do not feel loved nor lovable.

In their case the self-image inflicts the opposite demon upon them. It lets them operate with considerable social, affective and sexual confidence, but it strips them of confidence and stability in virtually every other area.

There are many lessons in all of this, not the least of which is that we need to express affection, we need to touch each other physically and we need to affirm each other more explicitly.

We need to express affection more, to stroke each other physically and emotionally into wholeness.

But we need also to realize that love is more than this. Even when there is not a satisfying affection in our lives, our eyes need not fill with tears every time we contemplate whether or not we are loved.

Sexuality Is More Than Sex

AS A CATHOLIC PRIEST, I am seldom taken seriously when I speak or write about sex. Invariably the reaction is: "What can you know about it, you don't have sex!"

I welcome that comment because it betrays the very attitude toward sex that I want to challenge, namely it identifies sexuality with having sex.

That is dangerously false and few things are as bad for us emotionally as that idea. Yet popularized Freudianism has given us this idea. It has made us believe that real love and friendship, at least of the heterosexual variety, depend upon having sexual relationships.

In brief it has made us believe that we cannot be whole without sex. Without sex, it is believed, we will end up sterile, dried up, old maids, "that way." Without sex our friendships and loves will be "platonic," anemic and unreal.

Concomitantly we nurse the idea that having sex is a panacea for all loneliness and emotional frustration. Sexology is too commonly a substitute for soteriology, meaning, happiness and sadness are identified with a fulfilling sexual relationship or its absence.

Because of this we suffer emotionally. When sexuality is synonymous with having sex, then, save brief moments, we live in much frustration and restless dissatisfaction. For all kinds of reasons we cannot sleep with everyone we feel drawn to and since friendship and love have become too much linked to sex we are constantly torn between infidelity and frustration.

The tragedy is not just that there is so much sexual and emotional infidelity around, but that, because of this, there is so little heterosexual friendship and love around (even within marriage).

It is no accident that in our culture it is easier to find a lover than a friend, just as it is no accident that, in our culture, virginity, celibacy, chastity within deep friendships and periodic abstinence within marriage are considered to be unrealistic or even positively harmful. Yet our deepest hungers and longings are for heterosexual relations beyond having sex. The ache is for men and women to come together as more than lovers.

This is not surprising. Sexuality is a huge thing. Our aches are multifarious. The word sex comes from the Latin *secare*, a word which literally means to cut off or divide from. We experience ourselves, at all levels, precisely as sexed, as cut off, divided from, unwhole. We ache for consummation, for a reuniting with some wholeness.

For this reason sexuality is always more than simply having sex. It is a dimension of our self-awareness. It is our eros, that irrepressible demand within us that we love and that energy within us that enables us to love. Through it we break out of the shells of our own egos and narcissism. Through it we seek contact, communication, wholeness, community, and creativity. Through sexuality we are driven and drawn beyond ourselves.

The sense of being sexed, cut off, is as present in us as our heartbeat. It permeates every level of our personalities and colors all of our relationships.

We are charged with sex. Physically, psychologically, spiritually, emotionally, intellectually and aesthetically we ache for union with something beyond ourselves. Maleness aches for femaleness, femaleness for the male. Sex colors all.

Yet having sex is merely one specific expression of our sexuality. It is simply one part, albeit a poignant one, of a much larger reality which we call sexuality. It is our contemporary inability to understand this that lies at the root of our obsession with sex. Around us, like an infectious virus, floats the idea that our personalities will expand or shrink depending upon whether we are having satisfying sex or not.

However, if sexuality is the drive for community, family, friendship, love and creativity, then whether we sleep alone or not is not so important. Community, family, friendship and creativity are. We can live with sex or without it, but we cannot live without community, family, friendship, and creativity. Our lives become warmer, more meaningful and more whole when these are there.

Conversely we grow colder and become bitter, sterile and dried up when they are absent. Our irrepressible longing is for community, family, friendship and creativity. Sexuality is the hunger and energy for them.

Having sex must always be understood within this context. It can help or harm. It helps when it fosters community, family, friendship and creativity. It harms when it blocks them. Given the contours of our personalities and our social lives, it appears impossible that, outside a relationship of love, permanent commitment, and marriage, having sex can foster community, family and friendship.

Experience tends to bear this out. Severing the tie between sex and marriage has not translated into more friendship, more community, more family and more love. We are lonelier than ever.

There is sex of the groin and sex of the heart. The former is full of dissatisfaction, exploitation, superficiality, schizophrenia and ultimately boredom (since, as W. H. Auden remarks, "All of us know the few things man as a mammal can do"). The latter is full of friendship, romance and passion. It is sex of the heart that cures loneliness and creates family, community and friendship.

We need, again, to learn the differences between sexuality and having sex.

No Salvation in Sexology

A NUN I know was traveling one day by air and found herself engaged in a conversation with a lively young man.

The young man had a myriad of questions, many concerning celibacy. At a certain point he remarked, "Looking at you, what intrigues me is that you are obviously a person who has a zest for life. Now think, Sister, how much richer your life could be if you also had sex!"

The nun simply replied, "Looking at you, what intrigues me is that you are obviously a person who is sincere and is searching for love. Love and sex aren't always the same thing. Now think how much richer your life could be if you understood that!"

This incident can help us understand why Christ chose to incarnate his sexuality in the manner that he did, namely as virgin.

By living and loving as virgin, Christ was not in any way trying to teach—as has sometimes been taught in the past—that consecrated celibacy is superior to marriage, or that there is something within sexual relations that works against the spiritual life. Rather, that the kingdom of God is more about the human heart than it is about the human groin.

Within Christ's perspective, the kingdom of God is about love, the nonexploitive meeting of human hearts. It consists of God and all persons of sincere will coming together in an all-in-one-heart-and-flesh community of life within which hearts are bonded in friendship, love, celebration and play-fulness.

Sex has a place within that, a beautiful and intensely poignant place. But it is not the kingdom, and to be the beautiful gift it was created to be it must always be linked to a chaste and permanent meeting of human hearts. It may never just be, as poet Margaret Atwood puts its, "a dentistry, the slick filling of aches and cavities."

Few messages are as urgently needed by our age as this challenge from Jesus to properly sort through the relation-ship between love and sex. We are a society which has all but turned sexology into a doctrine of salvation.

The classical language of salvation (which is the language of love)—"paying the price of sin," "giving until crucifix-ion," "suffering unto death"—has, for the largest part, been replaced by the language of sex. Love and salvation are talked about more in the language of Masters and Johnson than they are in the language of Christ.

Accordingly, for too many of us, love and salvation are seen more as the temporary mating of human bodies than as the permanent meeting of human hearts.

The price we pay for this is loneliness. It is no mere acci-dent that we are probably the loneliest society in the recorded history of humankind. We are also probably the most sexually active. Somehow, the increase in sexual activ-ity has not translated itself into an alleviation of loneliness and restlessness. For all our sexual freedom and sophistica-tion, we are caught up ever more deeply in restless chaos.

There is salvation in love alone. There is no justification in sex alone. The algebra of Christ's virginity is that, among other things, friendship and love, celebration and commu-nity, happiness and the kingdom, lie in the coming together of hearts. Sexuality contributes to the building up and the consummation of this community of hearts only when it helps lead to the joy and order that come from fidelity and chastity.

As Christians, therefore, we must incarnate our sexuality into the world in such a way that it constantly shows that love and the heart are the central realities of life and the kingdom.

We do this not by attempting to be asexual, or by setting the enjoyment of sex against the spiritual life, but rather by attempting to be sexual in the proper sense—namely in the way that Christ was. This can be done whether we are celibate or married.

If we are celibate and chaste, and yet are persons who are interpersonally unfearful, clearly sexual and warmly human, then we cannot help but challenge an age which, for all its searching, lives in loneliness and pain. Celibacy, if properly lived, can be an important way to keep alive, visible and in the flesh, that part of the incarnation which tells us that, when one is speaking of love, the human heart is the central organ.

Marriage, if properly lived out, is also excellently suited to teach this. Married persons imitate and help keep incarnate Christ's sexuality just as celibates do. Christ's virginity was not intended to set the joys of sex against the spiritual life. Sexually consummated love, if it is respectful, aesthetic, and linked to fidelity, is also a visible, enfleshed prolongation of the incarnation.

Since married love puts sexuality and love into their proper relationship, it visibly prolongs and transubstantiates Christ's sexuality.

It not only helps keep incarnate the life-creating power of sexuality, but it challenges powerfully the misconstrued notion that suggests that sex, disembodied from chastity and commitment, can in any way play a meaningful role in bring-ing final happiness and fulfillment into human life—or in-deed be of any use in the building up and consummation of God's kingdom.

How much richer our lives could be if we understood that!

Three Phases of Fantasy

WE HAVE ALWAYS BEEN taught that it is a bad thing to fantasize about sex, to have bad thoughts.

That may be true, but it is virtually impossible and perhaps unhealthy not to think about sex. We are so incurably sexual.

We ache for wholeness and, as we ache, we fantasize about that union which can end our aloneness. Our very condition spawns perpetual sexual temptations. That comes from God and is good.

Sex is a powerful, huge thing. Like breathing it is part and parcel of being alive, and like breathing it is necessary for life. It is not one isolated part of ourselves. Sex is co-extensive with our personalities in that it is a dimension of our self-awareness.

It is the way we seek contact, community and unity beyond ourselves and our separate egos. It is an energy, a power for loving, a merciless tension which pushes us outward.

As such it affects our whole being. All of our relationships and actions are sexually colored, tainted if you will, in some way. We do little, perhaps nothing, which is not affected, however inchoately, by the fact that we are cut off, divided, sexed.

But to say that sexuality seeps through into nearly all we think and do need not be a shameful confession, it can be a statement of health. Hence, sexual fantasizing can also be an indication of health rather than automatically a sign of self-ishness and perversion. But this needs considerable nuance:

Our sexuality is developmental and so too should be its attendant fantasies. What follows is an outline of certain discernible phases of sexual maturation and their consequences for sexual fantasizing. This schema is developed for the male sexual cycle but, with certain variations, is equally true for women.

The adolescent phase of sexuality begins with puberty and can last into the late twenties. At this stage, sexuality is predominantly genital. It can be indiscriminate in that its temptations and at times its actions can be frighteningly un-monogamous and it tends to be centered very much on plea-sure, physical and emotional.

One's fantasy life generally follows suit. Bad thoughts during this time are generally pretty bad, namely thoughts which are precisely genitally focused, which dwell on the bodily pleasures of sex.

But this phase normally gives way, during the mid to late twenties, or in some cases earlier, to a sexuality which yearns much more for intimacy than for sheer sexual pleasure or in-discriminate sexual union.

In this second stage sexuality becomes less raw, more dis-criminate, more romantic. The fantasy of intimacy, of em-brace, replaces cruder versions. At this stage sexual feelings widen to take in more aspects of the person.

At this stage too it begins to become more difficult to consider sexual fantasies simply as bad thoughts. Somehow the fantasy of embrace suggests more goodness and whole-ness than it suggests dirtiness and evil, unless of course it does not respect other persons' privacy, chastity, marriages and commitments.

But sexuality has yet a further phase. By one's mid to late thirties the issues of procreation, children and wider community begin to take center stage.

Sexuality at every level, body, mind, emotions, psyche, spirit, begins to demand that we give birth to something or, like Jephthah's daughter, it begins to mourn and bewail its virginity. Sexual union, even intimacy with some loved one, however deep and true, is no longer enough. Our sexuality now has hungers beyond that.

Our sexual energies, our erotic tensions, must now be poured out for a wider community. At this point in life all sexual pleasure and sexual intimacy becomes unhealthily narcissistic if it does not accept this.

And this is also true for our life of fantasy. As our sexuality widens and begins to be focused more on giving birth and on community, so too must our concomitant fantasies.

At this stage of our lives, I dare submit, we must cultivate sexual thoughts, but they must be fantasies of how we can pour our sexuality, the tension and energy inside us that is felt in our sense of being cut off and divided, into nurturing life, into new ways of producing life, into new ways of impregnating and being impregnated so as to help bring about new birth and new community.

We will always fantasize and we will always fantasize sexually. To be human is to have a fertile mind and imagination. To be sensitive is to have fertile feelings and fertile fantasies.

For better and for worse we are stuck with our "bad thoughts." When are they a share in God's hunger for a kingdom, something to be fostered, and when are they bad thoughts, something to be confessed? When are they healthy and when are they unhealthy?

Perhaps there are no clear answers to those questions.

However, even in a world in which the huge issues of social morality such as starvation, social injustice, abortion and the threat of nuclear war tend to make speculation on issues of private morality seem petty, these are worthwhile and ultimately important questions.

4

$\mathscr{B}$

KEEPING FIRE IN ONE'S EYES: LOSING AND RECOVERING INNOCENCE

There comes an hour in the afternoon when the child is tired of pretending; when he is weary of being a robber or a Red Indian. It is then that he torments the cat. There comes a time in the routine of an ordered civilization when the man is tired of playing at mythology and pretending that a tree is a maiden or that the moon made love to a man. The effect of staleness is the same everywhere; it is seen in all our drug-taking and dram-drinking and in every form of the tendency to increase the dose. Men seek stranger sins or more startling obscenities as stimulants to their jaded senses . . . They try to stab their nerves to life, as if it were with the knives of the priests of Baal. They are walking in their sleep and try to wake themselves with nightmares.

(G. K. CHESTERTON)

Keeping Fire in the Eyes

EVERY SO OFTEN we spend time in front of a mirror checking for signs of aging. We turn all the lights on and study ourselves. Are there wrinkles in our skin? Bags under our eyes? More grey hair? We scrutinize, examine. It's a proper enough exercise.

But we should be looking ourselves dead straight in the eyes when we do this exercise. In them we will see whether we are aging and whether or not there are any signs of senility.

Scrutinize and examine, look for signs of aging, but spend that time looking into your eyes. What do they reveal? Are they tired, unenthusiastic, cynical, lifeless, lacking in sparkle, hardened? Is the jealousy of Cain there?

Is there any fire there? Does passion still burn? Are they weary of experiencing, incapable of being surprised? Have they lost their virginity? Are they fatigued or excited? Is there still a young child buried somewhere behind them?

The real signs of senility are betrayed by the eyes, not the flesh. Drooping flesh means that we are aging physically, nothing more. Bodies age and die in a process as inevitable and natural as the law of gravity, but drooping eyes signify an aging spirit, a more deadly senility. That is less natural.

Spirits are meant to be forever young, forever childlike, forever virgin. They are not meant to droop or die.

But they can die through boredom and its child—cynicism. They can die through a lack of passion, through the illusion of familiarity, through a loss of childlikeness and virginity, and through a fatigue of the spirit we commonly call despair.

Despair is a curious thing. We despair not because we grow weary of the shortcomings and sufferings of life and, at last, find life too much to take. No. We despair for the opposite reason, namely, we grow weary of joy.

Joy lies in experiencing life as fresh, novel and primal, as a child does, with a certain purity of spirit. This type of joy is not pleasure, though there is pleasure in it.

Pleasure can be had without joy but that kind of pleasure is then the product of a lack of chastity in experiencing. That kind of pleasure, initially always experienced as a victory, as a throwing off of naïveté, a liberation, soon turns into defeat, that is, into dullness, boredom, loss and lack of passion. That kind of pleasure very soon becomes insipid, soya beans without salt, egg custard. Our palate loses its itch for tasting.

With that our enthusiasm dies and a fatigue of the spirit sets in. Our chief joy lies in an innocence and virginity in experiencing and when that joy is no longer sought, and we tire of pleasure, we grow listless, hardened, bitter, passionless. There is nothing left in us that is fresh and young.

Our eyes begin to show this. They lose their sparkle, their childlikeness. In her poignant novel, *Stone Angel*, Margaret Laurence describes her heroine, a lifeless and despairing lady named Hagar, studying herself in a mirror:

I stood for a long time, looking, wondering how a person could change so much . . . So gradually it happens. The face—a brown and leathery face that wasn't mine. Only the eyes were mine, staring as though to pierce the lying glass and get beneath to some true image, infinitely distant.

A good look in the mirror for most of us reveals the same, a lifeless face which is not really ours, and dull eyes, our own, but hidden deeply beneath a lying glass.

Our eyes and face, leathery, ossified, blank, distant, devoid of innocence and virginity; somewhere ("so gradually it happens") our fire went out!

What's to be done? My suggestion is that we take a good long look at ourselves in a mirror. Study the eyes, stare long and hard. Let what we see frighten us, frighten us enough to move us toward the road of unlearning and revirginization.

Look in a mirror, look at your face until some of the self-preoccupation, the cynicism, the pseudo-sophistication, and the unchastity and adultness drop away. Stare into your eyes until the lying glass breaks and you see there again the little boy or girl who once inhabited that space.

In that, wonder will be born, sparkle will return and, with it, a freshness and virginity that will make you feel young again.

Our eyes seldom grow tired, though they frequently get buried. It is the latter which causes the blank passionless stare. Bodies tire, but eyes are linked to spirits. They stretch and strain and sparkle in thirst before reality's turbid deluge. Eyes are always eager to see.

One of the great contrasts between Christianity and some other world religions has to do with the eyes. For example, the Buddhist saint is always depicted with his or her eyes shut, while the Christian saint always has them open. The Buddhist saint has a sleek and harmonious body but his or her eyes are heavy and sealed with sleep.

The medieval saint's body is wasted to its crazy-bone, but his or her eyes are frightfully alive, hungry, staring. The Buddhist is looking with a peculiar inwardness. The Christian's eyes are staring with frantic intentness outward.

The Real Loss of Virginity

SOME YEARS AGO, while giving a retreat, a lady came to me for confession. Her confession was long and sincere.

However, that sincerity and genuine contrition was constantly punctured by a cynicism, sarcasm and a background experience which caused her to be constantly questioning whether she wanted to be sincere and contrite.

She was very bright and very experienced. In virtually every sense of the word, she had been around. She was also very unhappy.

When we had finished she asked what I felt she needed to do. I suggested she should undergo a long and intensive process of revirginization. It was a suggestion which mildly shocked her, but it was what she really needed.

Though young, she had been almost everywhere, done almost everything, and had, in a way of speaking, sophisticated herself into a huge unhappiness. There was not a childlike bone in her body nor a childlike thought in her heart. She had lost most of her virginity.

That prescriptive counsel I gave her, revirginization, is a counsel which I judge more and more needs to be given to all of us and to our age in general. We are horribly unvirginal persons.

What is meant here?

Virginity is, in its deepest sense, not so much a past sexual history as a present attitude. Whether one is a virgin or not has less to do with his or her past sexual experiences as it has to do with the posture with which he or she meets reality.

What is the posture of virginity? It is comprised of three compenetrating elements:

First, virginity is the posture of a child before reality. A child has a very primitive, virginal spirit. In a child's heart and mind, and in a virgin's, there is a sense of newness, of experiencing for the first time. There is too a capacity to be surprised.

There is no illusion of familiarity and there is a natural "fear of God," love's fear, the fear that is the beginning of wisdom. Because of this, there is in the child or the virgin a sense of mystery, a sense that some things are sacred, untouchable, beyond manipulation.

Secondly virginity is living in a certain inconsummation, living with a desire for experience which is not fully satiated. To be a virgin is to live in tension, unfulfilled, longing, waiting for a time in the future when one will be fulfilled. The virgin does not prematurely enter the marriage bed. This is true not just in the area of sexuality, but in all of life.

Finally virginity is living in such a way that there are certain areas of our personality and life which are revered and sacred and which are then shared only within a context which fully respects that sacredness. For a virgin there is a certain chastity in experiencing, in all areas of life including the sexual.

Virginity opposes itself to promiscuity of all kinds. The virgin knows that the human heart, temple of the Holy Spirit that it is, is not cheap. As a precious gift it may only be trustfully given.

This posture, virginity, is natural in a child. However, here it is dependent upon certain factors which are themselves natural in children, namely ignorance, lack of experience, superstition, lack of opportunity, natural naïveté, and a lack of criticalness and practicalness.

As we grow older, as our critical faculties sharpen and as we experience more, we naturally lose much of our virginity. Partly this is necessary, natural and healthy—to be adult and naïve is not an ideal.

However, partially this loss of virginity is unnecessary and unhealthy. As was the case with the lady I described above, partly the loss of virginity is the result of giving in to the urge to experience indiscriminately, of stripping reality unduly of too many of its sacral dimensions, of illicitly breaking taboos (including sexual ones), and of letting impatience and despair drive us beyond chastity.

When this happens, and to a greater or lesser extent it happens in each of our lives, we develop a false familiarity with life and begin to live under the illusion of familiarity. This is the real loss of virginity, living in an unhealthy familiarity with life, others, sex. In this state, all real love, real romance, and all aesthetics in love, die. Ultimately the loss of virginity is characterized by a sophisticated unhappiness, an unchildlikeness which, while miserable, refuses to admit its own misery and its cause. That is one of the qualities of being in hell, to be miserable and to refuse to admit it.

With that comes a proclivity for the perverse. Why? Because as Chesterton so aptly puts it: "There comes an hour in the afternoon when the child is tired of pretending; when he is weary of being a robber or a Red Indian. It is then that he torments the cat."

Lately, as a culture, we have taken to tormenting the cat! How do we wake ourselves from the nightmare?

Saying Yes to Santa Claus

IF YOU ASK a naïve child: "Do you believe in Santa Claus?" he replies "Yes!" If you ask a bright child the same question, he replies "No!" However if you ask an even brighter child he replies "Yes!"

I have described above our need for "revirginization," our need again to say yes to the question of Santa Claus.

But how do we revirginize? How do we move toward a second naïveté?

We do it by touching the nerve of novelty, by purging ourselves of the illusion of familiarity. We must, as Chesterton put it, "Learn to look at things familiar until they look unfamiliar again."

We do this by making a deliberate and conscious effort at assuming the posture of a child before reality. We must work at regaining the primal spirit, a sense of wonder, the sense that reality is rich and full of mystery, that we do not yet understand and that we must read chastely, carefully, and discriminately, respecting reality's contours and taboos.

Concomitant with this effort comes the deliberate and conscious attempt at purging ourselves of all traces of cynicism, contempt, and all attitudes which identify mystery with ignorance, taboo with superstition, and romance and ideals with naïveté.

It also entails the willingness to put off gratification, to live in tension, to accept being unfulfilled. It entails, in every sense of the term, refusing to sleep with the bride before the wedding night. We revirginize by learning to wait—sexually, economically, emotionally, spiritually.

Finally revirginization and coming to second naïveté involves recovering again a certain chastity in experiencing. It involves recovering and respecting the sense that we ourselves and the reality around us are full of sacredness.

Perhaps the process of revirginization may best be described by two metaphors:

The image of weather revirginizing a geographical terrain: Imagine a geographical terrain that has been ravaged by natural disaster and despoiled by human beings. Its waters are dirty and polluted, its vegetation is dead and its natural beauty is destroyed.

However, given time and weather—the sun, the rains, the winds, the storms, the frost and snow—it, in a manner of speaking, revirginizes. Its waters again grow clear and pure, its vegetation returns to life and eventually its natural beauty returns. In a manner of speaking, its chastity returns, making it again "virgin territory."

So too with our hearts and minds: as soon as we stop despoiling them through the illusion of familiarity and indiscriminate experience, they too regain, gradually, their virginity and begin again to blush in the wonder of knowing and loving. A chastity in knowing and loving returns.

The image of fetal darkness: Imagine the gestation process of a human being in the womb. The process begins with a mere egg, a cellular speck which is being gestated, formed, cared for, shaped by things around it and nourished by a reality infinitely larger than itself. The process takes place in darkness, in a dark peace. Eventually the child has grown sufficiently and emerges for the first time.

The sheer overwhelmingness of the mystery of reality is so overpowering that it takes a long time, years of time, for the senses and mind to harden sufficiently for the child to even begin to understand. Initially the child simply looks and wonders.

So too the process of coming to second naïveté, of revirginizing. We must truly be born again. We must, metaphorically speaking, make a recessive journey, a voyage to the sources, to the fetal darkness of the womb to be reduced to a mere egg, to be gestated anew in darkness (in the darkness of an understanding that understands more by not understanding than by understanding) so that we can again open our eyes to a new awareness that is so wild, so startling, so agnostic, and so overpowering that we are unable to name and number, but are reduced, as it were, to having to ponder and to wonder.

G. K. Chesterton expresses this beautifully in a poem:

> When all my days are ending
> And I have no song to sing,
> I think I shall not be too old
> To stare at everything;
> As I stared once at a nursery door
> Or a tall tree and a swing . . .
> (CHESTERTON, *A Second Childhood*)

May we never grow too old, too sophisticated, too unchildlike, too unvirginal, to stare at everything as we "stared once at a nursery door."

Don't Kill Santa Claus Too Soon

IN HIS BEST-SELLING BOOK, *The Closing of the American Mind*, Allan Bloom describes a contemporary professor who sees his task as that of setting people free by breaking taboos:

> He reminded me of the little boy who gravely informed me when I was four that there was no Santa Claus, who wanted me to bathe in the brilliant light of truth . . . My informant about Santa Claus was just showing off, proving his superiority to me . . . Think of all we learn about the world from men's belief in Santa Clauses, and all we learn about the soul from those who believe in them. By contrast, merely methodological excision from the soul of the imagination (which lets us believe in this kind of thing) does not promote knowledge of the soul, it only lobotomizes it, cripples its powers.

The breaking of taboos, the death of an innocence, however naïve, what does this do to the human soul?

I was raised in a time when there was an emphasis on chastity. There were a lot of taboos. Many things were not permitted and among many of the important things that were, dating, friendship, marriage, sex, there was a certain protocol that had to be observed; a certain caution, a waiting, a string of taboos, and a proper way in which a thing was to be accomplished.

We call it chastity. Not everyone was chaste, of course, but the ideal was basically agreed upon.

Today this has changed. Far from being thought of as positive, as the key to all experience, chastity is associated with being inhibited, repressed, timid and naïve.

The push is to break taboos, to experience more things and to experience them earlier.

Few persons, I am sure, would deny this. Many, I suspect, will however deny what I am about to say, namely that a lot of the emotional chaos, meaninglessness, and deep despair that is ungluing the Western psyche comes, in the end, from a lack of chastity. Let me explain.

The biggest crisis within our culture is not economic, but psychic. Emotional unrest, deep dis-ease, sexual pathos, the sense of loss, of meaninglessness, of death, these are the deep cancers in Western society.

Human goodness remains and God's unconditional love will, ultimately, wash all things clean. But if our souls are not going to the devil they certainly are dying to youth, inno-cence, enthusiasm and passion.

As Bloom puts it in his book, our eros has gone lame.

Even as we grow emotionally more chaotic and more deeply restless, the eros of our youth and the enthusiasm for true sexuality are dead.

We are no longer fired into life by a madness that comes from our incompleteness and lets us believe that we can re-cover our wholeness through the embrace of another, the perpetuity of our seed, and the contemplation of God.

Instead we are tired, erotically fatigued, lame. We have already been there! We have had a look! There is a deadness within the Western soul.

How does this link to chastity, or lack of it?

Already a generation ago, Albert Camus, an atheistic

writer, commented "Chastity alone is connected with personal progress. There is a time when moving beyond it is a victory—when it is released from its moral imperatives. But this quickly becomes a defeat afterwards" (quoted in P. Rieff, *The Triumph of the Therapeutic*).

What Camus is suggesting is that the feeling of emotional despair that is so pervasive in our culture is a result of a lack of chastity. To understand this, however, we need better to understand what chastity is.

Chastity is normally defined as something to do with sex, namely a certain innocence, purity, discipline, or even celibacy regarding sex. This is too narrow.

Chastity is, first, not primarily a sexual concept. It has to do with the limits and appropriateness of all experiencing, sexual experience included.

To be chaste means to experience things, all things, respectfully and to drink them in only when we are ready for them. We break chastity when we experience anything irreverently or prematurely. This is what violates either another's or our own growth.

It is the lack of chastity in experiencing, irreverence and prematurity, that lobotomizes the soul.

Experience can be good or bad. It can help glue the psyche together or tear it apart. It can produce joy or chaos. Travel, study, achievement, sex, exposure to newness, the breaking of taboos, all can be good, if experienced reverently and at their proper time.

Conversely they can tear the soul apart (even when they are not wrong in themselves) when they are not drunk in chastely, namely at a pace that respects fully both others' and our own growth.

Always look carefully at any taboo. Always link learning to integration, epistemology to morality, experience to chastity. There is much danger in killing Santa Claus too soon.

Staring Chaos in the Face

WE LIVE IN pain and division. In the world, in the church and within ourselves, there is much anger, hatred and bitterness.

It seems ever harder to live at peace with each other, to be calm, to have simple joy within our lives and not to alienate someone just by being.

Within ourselves, despite the fact that we have virtually every practical reason to be happy—friends, health, material affluence—we experience anger, jealousy and woundedness. Seldom are we satisfied. Seldom are we truly free of bitterness, anger and feelings of being slighted and overlooked. Very seldom are we fully at peace with life and with others.

Beyond this, we live in a world that is full of painful division. It has its own wounds.

Poverty, social injustice, the inequality of men and women, racism, abortion, sexual exploitation, narcissistic yuppies, untrustworthy political leaders, and simply millions of persons caught up in excessive self-interest.

It is hard for us, as adults in our world, to simply love, be understanding, and be at peace with others and with life. We are wounded, within and without. The temptation is toward bitterness, anger, withdrawal and paranoia. That is the road to hell because bitterness is hell.

What is needed to stop our slide toward this is reconciliation, at every level.

What is reconciliation? It is reality that admits many levels.

Here I want to speak of reconciliation as personal healing, as a coming inside of ourselves to a new wholeness and a renewed sense of childlike joy.

Reconciliation, at this level, involves many things. First it involves the recognition of our woundedness, our neuroses, our bitterness, our narcissism and narrow loyalties, and simply our lack of joy.

Just as for an alcoholic there can be no real change before there is the basic admittance of the conditions of helplessness and need, so too in our struggle to come to personal healing. There can be no healing until we admit sickness. And we are ill: compulsive, angry, competitive, bitter, narcissistic, cynical, humorless, paranoid, self-pitying, jealous, somber and joyless.

The roots of this woundedness stretch deep into our past, and beyond our past into the history of the world. We are not just part of the chain of love, but are likewise part of a chain of neuroses and wound that stretches back, ultimately, to Adam and Eve.

We can sometimes point to certain events and persons that have hurt us deeply and blame much of our pain on them. However these events and persons themselves point still further back to distant events and persons that wounded them.

There was some original sin—and life has not been harmonious, nor seemed fair, ever since.

Reconciliation begins when we truly admit this. So long as we pretend otherwise, it is not even meaningful to use the word. When we claim our woundedness, however, we are brought face to face with our own helplessness, our need, our need for God.

Then, as Henri Nouwen puts it, our hearts "become the

place where the tears of God and the tears of God's children can merge and become tears of hope" (*Love in a Fearful Land*, 1986).

The first step in real reconciliation is the tearful acknowledgment of our woundedness, our helplessness, our sin. In this admission is a painful dying and a joyous rebirth.

Ashes make the best fertilizer. Tears wash away sin. Honesty induces the labor that gives birth to conversion.

When we cry honest tears, we are flooded with the desire to pray, to forgive, to serve others, to build a just social order, to live more moral lives, to love beyond resentment and bitterness. That is the movement toward reconciliation and joy.

Why? Because searing honesty brings us face to face with our own woundedness and helplessness; our helplessness, in turn, brings us face to face with a redeeming God.

In that encounter, we learn that we are loved sinners. Gratitude is born. A genuine sanctity follows.

Novelist Iris Murdoch states that to be a saint is nothing less than to be warmed and vitalized by gratitude.

Gratitude is the key to all. We come to personal healing and to reconciliation with others to the exact extent that we are warmed and vitalized by gratitude.

To rid ourselves of resentment, bitterness, jealousy and paranoia requires a powerful fire. Only the gratitude that flows from knowing that we are loved, loved despite wound and sin, is a large enough flame to burn wound from our lives.

The rest follows: When we are vitalized by gratitude we will automatically move toward deeper prayer, wider loyalties and a more embracing heart.

Reconciliation begins when we stare our chaos in the

face. In that, we will be brought face to face with our helplessness and our need for God. Prayer will then begin, crying out from the very depths of our being.

We will be laid bare and will realize that we are loved sinners, in solidarity with other loved sinners like ourselves. Gratitude, reconciliation and healing will follow.

Be Brave, Admit Your Sinfulness

AFTER CONCLUDING a confession within which she had admitted to some rather serious things, a lady asked me, "What would you call those things? My neuroses? My woundedness? My struggle areas? My immaturities?"

Half-jokingly, I answered, "Call them sin! Afford to them and to yourself the dignity of a rich and timeless symbol."

Her confession had been honest and she was not, in posing that question, trying to evade responsibility or guilt. Yet, within her, there was something which made her hesitate to simply say "I sinned, I am a sinner."

In that hesitation, she is a child of our age. Today, unless we are speaking of corporate or systematic evil, there is a general hesitancy to use the word sin.

It is rare that we hear someone simply and humbly say, beyond any reference to circumstances or excuse: "I've sinned. There aren't any excuses . . . outside of being human."

We are poorer for not being able to say that.

First of all we are poorer because our sense of sin is connected with our sense of love. To sin is to betray—in love. To have lost a sense of personal sin is to have lost a sense of being personally and deeply loved.

Lovers know that their immaturities, woundedness and neuroses play a part in their struggles. They also know that, ultimately, there is something called betrayal, sin.

Secondly, more superficially, not to speak of ourselves as sinners is to lower the symbolic hedge under which we live. Bluntly put, psychological symbols—neuroses, immaturity, woundedness—do not link our actions to anything interesting, rich or timeless. The symbol of sin does.

A sin, in the end, can be ever so much more interesting and rich than a neurosis or an immaturity. Daniel Berrigan stated sarcastically that when the obituary for our age is written it will tell future generations that our age died of "nothing more serious than moral acne, hemorrhoids of the spirit."

I would like to think that our faults have more dignity than that! The symbol of sin links our faults to the weaknesses of all who have ever struggled and with all who will ever struggle. A sense of sin grounds us, humbly, in history.

More seriously, however: to admit that we sin gives us the space to be honest and a place within which to receive forgiveness.

When we refuse to admit that we sin we are forced to be dishonest because, in the end, no one can honestly stand before God and others and not have to say: "I am weak. I do things I shouldn't. The good I want to do, I cannot. The evil I want to avoid, I end up doing. I need forgiveness."

Not to say this, is to lie. Not to admit sin forces us to rationalize, to give excuses, to project blame, and to overemphasize psychological and sociological influences on our behavior.

We see this already in the Adam and Eve story. Confronted by God after their sin, they are unable simply to admit sin. Instead we see the proclivity for rationalization: "The woman you gave me offered me the fruit! The devil tempted me!"

Had there been, then, the simple honesty to admit sin, human history might have been different. Instead of crying out for redemption, Adam and Eve burrowed themselves more deeply into their own woundedness.

The same is true for us. When we lie and rationalize we refuse to stand in the space within which we can receive forgiveness and we retreat more deeply into what is not best in us.

It is when we can stand before God and others as the publican did and say in the face of our betrayals, "These things are wrong. I shouldn't be doing this . . . but I can't help myself," that we can receive the forgiveness that washes us clean. Forgiveness does not wash away neuroses or immaturities. It washes away sin.

It is when we humbly and simply own our sin that we take our place among God's broken, the ones Jesus came to save, and are given the chance to start again, new, fresh, loved.

A man I know is fond of expressing his displeasure with his own moral failures by saying: "That was incredibly stupid . . . but it seemed like a good idea at the time!" That's a contemporary form of the publican's prayer. There's an honesty in that which allows him to accept forgiveness.

Another person I know, a lady who has been coming to me for the sacrament of reconciliation for some time, always begins her confession with the beautiful phrase: "I am a loved sinner."

In that expression, she keeps in correct balance the most important truths of humanity: We are sinners and we are loved in spite of it.

To admit sin sets us free to receive love under the only

condition it can be truly offered. To acknowledge that we are loved, in spite of sin, sets us free from false guilt and self-hatred.

Martin Luther had precisely this in mind when he so wisely said: "Sin bravely!"

When Sinners Rationalize

SEVERAL YEARS AGO, after the pope had been heckled during his visit in Holland, a Belgian newspaper ran an editorial which commented as follows: The difference between the Dutch and the Belgians can be seen in their separate reactions to the pope. In Holland people do not keep the commandments but they still want to be saints, so they demand that the commandments be changed. In Belgium we do not keep the commandments, either, but we know we are not saints and so we admit it and ask for redemption.

Perhaps there is bias in that comment as it relates to the differences between the Dutch and the Flemish, but it has insight in another way.

Our culture struggles with honesty, with admitting weakness. Much within us and around us invites us to rationalize, to make excuses, to demand that standards be changed or reintegrated because we cannot live up to them.

Less and less, even in prayer and confession, do we find searing honesty and contrition.

This proclivity to rationalize and not admit weakness and sin is, singularly, the most deadly temptation facing each of us. Failure to admit weaknesses and acknowledge our sin as sin is infinitely more damaging than weakness and sin themselves.

Failure in self-honesty is the start of the sin against the Holy Spirit, the only sin that can never be forgiven.

We are familiar with Christ's warning that there exists a

sin, a certain blasphemy against the Holy Spirit, which can never be forgiven. What is this sin?

Simply put, it is the sin of lying to oneself until one becomes so warped that one believes one's own lie. Falsehood becomes truth. The reason this sin cannot be forgiven is not that God does not want to forgive it, but rather that the person no longer sees the need for forgiveness. Living in darkness is seen as living in light; sin is seen as grace; perversion as virtue.

The person living in this state feels a certain disdain for what is genuinely virtuous, innocent and happy. She or he would not accept forgiveness were it offered.

This sin begins always with rationalization, with the failure to admit to sin. And much within ourselves and our world feeds this temptation to rationalize, to take ourselves off the hook, to make ourselves look good by denying our weakness and sin.

We see this everywhere, in our tendency to avoid confession of all kinds, in our inability to take personal responsibility for our own unhappiness, and in our tendency not to admit our moral misery. We see it too in our inability to be searingly contrite in confession—whether in a church or elsewhere.

More and more, our confessions are more protests against moral authority and rationalizations than they are honest admissions of simply being human and sinning. More common than genuine contrition is anger toward moral authority, especially toward the church.

In my opinion this does not augur well. The heart of anger, as someone once wisely stated, is a rebellion against what it means to be human.

Too rare, today, is the confession of the publican: "I'm a

sinner! I'm a mess! I am morally inept, unable to live what I believe. I do dumb things because I am weak. There's no excuse. And, God, I'm miserable, be merciful!"

More common is the tendency to blame the church, its moral authorities, or our past religious training for the fact that we suffer from guilt and un-freedoms which leave us less than happy.

Ruth Burrows, in her *Guidelines for Mystical Prayer* (Sheed & Ward, 1976), states:

> I am shocked to see how little contrition, searing contrition, features in our living and dying. Only a saint can afford to die the death of a saint. The rest of us need to go out as sinners in our own eyes and in the eyes of our entourage, and our peace must come from trust in God's goodness, not the complacent but unexpressed assumption that we lived for God.

She goes on to tell the stories of two nuns with whom she lived. The first was a sister who was not faithful to her life of prayer. She lived in mediocrity for most of her life. However, she admitted it. She never played games pretending she was anything other than what she was—mediocre. As she grew older she made more of an effort at fidelity, but habits die hard and she died before she fully succeeded. But she died a happy death, a sinner asking God to forgive her a life of human weakness.

The second sister also lived a life of mediocrity and infidelity in charity and prayer. Unlike the first sister, however, she never admitted this. To herself and to others, she postured saintliness. The result was a sad lie; harmful most of all to herself.

Only a saint can afford to live and die that role. The rest of us must live and die in searing contrition, sinners asking God and others to forgive us a life of weakness.

In such honesty lies redemption. In anything less honest lie seeds which, if allowed to grow, lead one to begin to blaspheme against the Holy Spirit.

Taking the Sting Out of Life

Mother tended to become riveted on what she felt as a personal slight or insult but she would not discuss it with you . . . She silently brooded over the incident and carried it with her inside. She remembered only the insult, however accidental, and it grew as time passed.

Usually such a misunderstanding fades away with time. But for Mother, the process was the opposite. She clung to the image of the old hurt, to her own secret image as the deprived somehow cheated and unloved person.

That image was a bottomless pit into which you could pour years of loving, kindness, and attempts at reconciliation without visible results. It failed to erase the one mistake.

It put you at a permanent disadvantage. Your unpremeditated error in judgment became part of a larger aberration that existed privately in the far reaches of her childhood deprivation, her own alienation and loneliness, her insatiable need for love.

There just wasn't enough love in the whole world to fill her need. She didn't allow enough space for other human beings to be themselves and give her anything real. She demanded such constant reassurance of devotion that she left no room for love. It was impossible to satisfy her.

Over the years, most of the people who really did

love her, in spite of her demands, were pushed away because she seemed unable to accept others as totally separate from herself. (Christina Crawford, *Mommie Dearest*, Mayflower, 1980)

What is it that I want from Uncle William? I want some hesitation at the door, as if he isn't sure he is welcome. I want him to take me aside and tell me he knows that he has done me harm.

I want him to sit, if he must sit, at my table, silent and absorbed. I don't demand that he be hounded; I don't even want him to confess. I simply want him to know, as I want the Irish sailor to know, that a wrong has been done me.

I want to believe that they remember it with at least regret. I know that things cannot be taken back, the forced embrace, the caresses brutal underneath the mask of courtship, but what I do want taken back are the words, spoken by these two men, that suggest that what they did was all right, no different from what other men have done, that it's all the same, the touch of men and women; nothing of desire or consent has weight, body parts touch body parts; that's all there is.

I want them to know that because of them I cannot ever feel about the world the way I might have felt had they never come near me. (Mary Gordon, "Violation," in *Temporary Shelter*)

Hurt, resentment, the inability to really forgive and forget, the hook of the past in our present, the universal condition of need, the chain of neuroses that stretches back to Adam and Eve, the need for a redemptive healing embrace from outside us are what is captured in these quotes.

In the first of them Christina describes her mother, Joan Crawford, and her mother's inability to move beyond her childhood hurts. It is a haunting statement because all of us, in some way, share her condition; present hurts invariably touch the deeper recesses where lie the wounds of our childhood. We fill with paranoia and resentment far too easily.

Mary Gordon, in her powerful essay on sexual violation, first describes how she was twice sexually violated; once by an anonymous Irish sailor and another time by her Uncle William. Now, years later, she finds that feelings of resentment and sadness still fill her at times and rob her ordinary life of some of its full richness for enjoyment.

As she is writing this essay she is reflecting upon the feelings that have been triggered in her by the announcement that her Uncle William is coming with her parents for lunch at her house. Trying to pinpoint what is still unresolved within her after all the years, she summarizes all in one line: "because of them I cannot ever feel about the world the way I might have felt had they never come near me."

An entire metaphysics of resentment is contained in that single line: Every hurt, every violation, every undeserved bruise gives us a new way of knowing, a wisdom and a bitterness. After every wound we begin to feel about the world differently than we would have—had this not come near us.

That is an enlightening insight, but to what purpose?

Freud held strongly that self-knowledge brings freedom, knowing why we act in a certain way helps us to act in a different way. Perhaps that is not as true as Freud supposes, but, as every recovering alcoholic can vouch for, self-knowledge is a necessary starting point. Until one looks in a mirror honestly nothing much will change.

Hence I offer these quotes as a mirror. In it we see ourselves, our woundedness, our resentment, our neurotic inability to love simply and joyfully, our paranoia, our propensity for self-pity, our insatiable need for reassurance and our limitless capacities for hurting each other.

But this is not meant to be a stoic mirror, within which one sees all the elements realistically, but does not resolve the conflict. Rather it is meant to be the mirror of humility within which we recognize our connectedness with everything and everybody.

If we can do this honestly then we will begin to feel the ache for redemption and we will have the humility to reach out for the embrace which can make all things well and make the fire and rose one; and enable us to meet the universe and each other with a sympathy born of the fact that life, for everyone, is an arduous and difficult struggle.

5

PRAYER AND THE MONASTICISM OF DAILY LIFE

It takes only a slight shift of emphasis, and
the point of aloneness in dynamic stillness
becomes the point of consummate union.

(David Steindl-Rast)

The Monasticism of Daily Life

DAVID STEINDL-RAST has commented that leisure is not the privilege of those who have time, but rather the virtue of those who give to each instant of life the time it deserves.

That is a valuable insight, especially today when everywhere life seems dominated by the constraints of time. Always, it seems, there is not enough time. Our lives are dominated by pressure, the rat race, demands which are all-absorbing. The plant has to run and, by the time that is taken care of, there is no time or energy for anything else.

And we are conscious of our pathological busyness. We know that life is passing us by and we are so preoccupied with the business of making a living and the duties of family and community that only rarely is there any time to actually live. It seems that there is never any unpressured time, unhurried time, undesignated time, leisure time, time to smell the flowers, simply to luxuriate in being alive. We lament about this over our coffee but are unable effectively to change anything.

Is there something frighteningly wrong with our lives? Is there a need to drastically change our lifestyles?

Perhaps. Obviously in our lives there is too little family time, prayer time, celebration time and simply restful time. But we are also compounding our problem through misunderstanding. Philosophies of "taking time to smell the flowers" have sometimes led us to understand leisure precisely as the privilege of the rich and unoccupied. What Steindl-Rast challenges us to do is to understand time correctly.

Time is a gift. When T. S. Eliot says, "Time, not our time," he is pointing out that there needs to be a certain detachment from time, a certain monasticism in our lives.

In monasteries life is regulated by a bell. Monks and nuns know that time is not their own, that when the bell rings they must drop whatever they are doing and move on to what is being asked of them next. When the bell rings, St. Benedict said, the monk must put down his pen without crossing his "t" or dotting his "i." He must move on, not necessarily because he feels like doing something else, but because it is time—time to eat, or pray, or work, or study, or sleep. Monks' lives are regulated by a bell, not because they do not have watches and alarm clocks, but to remind them, always, that time is not their own and that there is a proper time to do things. Monks do not get to sleep, eat, pray, work or relax when they feel like it, but when it is time to do those things.

There is an astonishing parallel between that and what happens in our own lives and we can be helped by understanding it. There is an inbuilt monasticism to our lives. We too, at least for the more active years, are called to practice a certain asceticism regarding time—to have our lives regulated by "the bell."

In our case "the bell" takes a different form, though its demands are the same as those of the bell in a monastery. In our case the bell is an alarm clock and the dictates of our daily lives: a quick breakfast, a commute to work (carrying sandwiches for lunch), staying home with small children, demands at work or at home, driving kids for lessons, dealing with them and their demands, household chores, cooking, laundry, taking out garbage, calling in a plumber, church on Sundays. Like monks we sleep, rise, eat, pray and work, not necessarily when we would like to but when it is time.

And this is true, not just for our daily routine but as well for the seasons of our lives. We go to school, we prepare for a career, we enter the work force, are tied down with kids, mortgage payments, car payments, and the demands of family and work, not necessarily because we always feel like it, but because it is that time in our lives. The play of children and the leisure of retirement come before and after that season.

During all of the most active years of our lives we are reminded daily, sometimes hourly, that time is not our own; we are monks practicing a demanding asceticism.

There will not always be time to smell the flowers and we are not always poorer for that fact. Monasticism has its own spiritual payoffs. To be forced to work, to be tied down with duties, to have to get up early, to have little time to call your own, to be burdened with the responsibility of children and the demands of debts and mortgages, to go to bed exhausted after a working day is to be in touch with our humanity. It is too an opportunity to recognize that time is not our own and that any mature spirituality makes a distinction between the season of work and the sabbath, the sabbatical, the time of unpressured time.

Most important of all, recognizing in our duties and pressures the sound of the monastic bell actually helps us to smell the flowers, to give to each instant of our lives the time it deserves—and not necessarily the time I feel like giving it. We are better for the demands that the duties of state put on us, despite constant fatigue. Conversely, the privileged who have all the time in the world are worse off for that, despite their constant opportunity to smell the flowers.

Monks have secrets worth knowing—and the pedagogy of a monastic bell is one of them.

Monasticism and the Playpen

THERE IS A TRADITION, strong among spiritual writers, that we will not advance within the spiritual life unless we pray at least an hour a day privately.

I was stressing this one day in a talk, when a lady asked how this might apply to her, given that she was at home with young children who demanded her total attention.

"Where would I ever find an uninterrupted hour each day?" she moaned. "I would, I am afraid, be praying with children screaming and tugging at my legs."

A few years ago, I might have been tempted to point out to her that if her life was that hectic then she, of all people, needed time daily, away from her children, for private prayer among other things. As it was I gave her different advice:

"If you are at home alone with small children whose needs give you little uninterrupted time, then you don't need an hour of private prayer daily. Raising small children, if it is done with love and generosity, will do for you exactly what private prayer does."

Left unqualified, that is a dangerous statement. It suggests in fact that raising children is a functional substitute for prayer.

However, in making the assertion that a certain service—in this case raising children—can in fact be prayer, I am bolstered by the testimony of contemplatives themselves.

Carlo Carretto, one of our century's best spiritual writers, spent many years in the Sahara Desert by himself, praying. Yet he once confessed that he felt that his mother, who spent nearly thirty years raising children, was much more contemplative than he was, and less selfish.

If that is true, and Carretto suggests that it is, the conclusion we should draw is not that there was anything wrong with his long hours of solitude in the desert, but that there was something very right about the years his mother lived an interrupted life amid the noise and demands of small children.

John of the Cross, in speaking about the very essence of the contemplative life, writes: "But they, O my God and my life, will see and experience your mild touch, who withdraw from the world and become mild, bringing the mild into harmony with the mild, thus enabling themselves to experience and enjoy you" (*The Living Flame of Love*, Burns & Oates, 1977).

In this statement John suggests there are two elements that are crucial to the contemplative's experience of God, namely withdrawal from the world and the bringing of oneself into harmony with the mild.

Although his writings were intended primarily for monks and contemplative nuns who physically withdraw from the world so as to seek a deeper empathy with it, his principles are just as true for those who cannot withdraw physically.

Certain vocations, for example raising children, offer a perfect setting for living a contemplative life. They provide a desert for reflection, a real monastery.

The mother who stays at home with small children experiences a very real withdrawal from the world. Her existence is certainly monastic. Her tasks and preoccupations remove her from the centers of social life and from the centers of important power. She feels removed.

Moreover her constant contact with young children, the

mildest of the mild, gives her a privileged opportunity to be in harmony with the mild and learn empathy and unselfishness.

Perhaps more so even than the monk or the minister of the Gospel, she is forced, almost against her will, to mature. For years, while she is raising small children, her time is not her own, her own needs have to be put into second place, and every time she turns round some hand is reaching out demanding something. Years of this will mature most anyone.

It is because of this that she does not need, during this time, to pray for an hour a day. And it is precisely because of this that the rest of us, who do not have constant contact with small children, need to pray privately daily.

We, to a large extent, do not have to withdraw. We can often put our own needs first. We can claim some of our own time. We do not work with what is mild. Our worlds are professional, adult, cold and untender. Outside of prayer we run a tremendous risk of becoming selfish and bringing ourselves into harmony with what is untender.

Monks and contemplative nuns withdraw from the world to try to become less selfish, more tender, and more in harmony with the mild. To achieve this they pray for long hours in solitude.

Mothers with young children are offered the identical privilege: withdrawal, solitude, the mild. But they do not need the long hours of private prayer—the demands and mildness of the very young are a functional substitute.

Fear of Tenderness Stifles the Soul

"THE PERSON who will not have a softening of the heart will eventually have a softening of the brain!" That warning, issued by G. K. Chesterton more than half a century ago, is particularly relevant for today, a time when virtually everything conspires against tenderness and softness.

Everywhere today the atmosphere is one of professionalism, efficiency, toughness, competitiveness and lean strength. Workplaces, and at times even our homes and church circles, leave little room for softness, be it inefficiency, sentiment or fat.

Even to insert a call for any tenderness and softness to somehow tone this down is to endanger one's status and respect. Our world has a very restricted place for what is unprofessional, sentimental, inefficient, fat, soft and fragile. Toughness and achievement are what get respect.

For this reason, we often experience our places of work and even our homes as being cold and somewhat brutal. But when we feel this coldness, what we are actually experiencing is our own intimidation. Our fear of being seen as soft, fat, childish, and as unable to handle pressure and meet certain standards of toughness and efficiency pushes us to make every kind of sacrifice rather than let ourselves be so judged.

This should not be so but in fact most often is. Ideally we should not allow ourselves to be thus intimidated but, most often, we do. The fact is that we generally do live and work within an atmosphere that is cold and unfeeling.

Given this, it is all too easy for us to become embittered, cold and competitive ourselves. This happens gradually, imperceptibly, like the process of aging and the greying of hair. We look in the mirror each day and think we look the same. Then one day we look at an old photograph of ourselves and we are shocked at how much we have changed.

If we could see old photographs of ourselves which somehow indicated eagerness of spirit, spontaneity, hospitality, compassion, and simple joy and zest for life, many of us, I suspect, would be shocked at how much we have changed, hardened, through the years. The coldness, untenderness, and hardness that was so long outside us, is now, in a large measure, inside, in our eyes, in our actions, and, sadly, often enough in our hearts. So gradually it happens. We change, harden, become the type of persons we would not choose to be friends with ourselves.

Given this, perhaps the most important prayer moments we can have each day are those moments which soften the heart, moments which bring us back to eagerness of spirit, hospitality, compassion and childlike joy. To have a tender moment is to pray.

Praying is more than just saying prayers. We are asked to "pray always." This implies that we need to be praying even when we are not formally saying prayers.

To pray always, as Jesus says, implies that we read the signs of the times, that we look at the conspiracy of accidents which shape our lives and read in these the finger and providence of God. The language of God is the experience that God writes into our lives. To pray means to read our lives religiously.

Perhaps the most important way in which we need to do this today is to pick up, read religiously, and see as grace and

prayer those moments which somehow soften the hea[rt], [mo]-
ments which put us in touch with our vulnerability, our tenderness, our sense of compassion and hospitality, and our
connectedness with each other and our common struggle.
We share a common heart and a common struggle. To become aware of that is to soften the heart.

The world can be hard and, if we are not careful, if we do
not massage the tender moment as prayer, we will harden too,
becoming as untender, cold, and inhospitable as the world
itself.

William Wordsworth observed that a person often seems
cold when she or he is only hurt. I suspect too many of us radiate this coldness for precisely that reason.

We need to pray by picking up the tender moment and
letting its grace soften us.

What constitutes the tender moment? Anything in life
that helps make us aware of our deep connectedness with
each other, of our common struggle, our common wound,
our common sin, and our common need for help: the suffering face of another which mirrors our own pain, the sense of
our physical mortality, the acceptance of our own sin, the
beauty of nature, the eagerness and innocence of children,
the fragility of the aged, and, of course, not least, moments
of intimacy, of friendship, of celebration, of every kind of
shared joy, pain or vulnerability.

John of the Cross suggested that the function of solitude
is "to bring the mild into harmony with the mild." Moments
which make us mild are deep moments of prayer.

We need such moments badly or a cold and brutal world
will make us cold and brutal. We need, daily, to pick up the
tender moment.

Chesterton also said:

The swiftest things are the softest things. A bird is active because a bird is soft. A stone is helpless, because a stone is hard. The stone must by its own nature go downwards, because hardness is weakness. A bird can of its nature go upwards, because fragility is force. (*Orthodoxy*)

Just Too Busy to Bow Down

THEOLOGIAN JAN WALGRAVE commented that our present age constitutes a virtual conspiracy against the interior life. That is a gentle way of saying that, within our culture, distraction is normal, prayer and solitude are not. There is little that is contemplative within our culture and within our lives.

Why is this? We are not, by choice or ideology, a culture set against solitude, interiority and prayer. Nor are we, in my opinion, more malicious, pagan or afraid of interiority than past ages. Where we differ from the past is not so much in badness as in busyness, in hurriedness. We do not think contemplatively because we never quite get around to it.

Perhaps the most apt metaphor to describe our hurried and distracted lives is that of a car wash. When you pull up to a car wash, you are instructed to leave your motor running, to take your hands off the steering wheel and to keep your foot off the brake. The idea is that the machine itself will suck you through.

For most of us, that is just what our typical day does to us, it sucks us through. We now have radios within our alarm clocks which go off before the alarm actually wakes us. Hence we are already stimulated before we are fully awake.

Then we rise to a radio to shower and dress and ready ourselves for work, stimulated by news, music, commentary. Breakfast and the drive to work follow the same pattern. We listen to the radio, engage in conversation, plan our agenda, stimulated and preoccupied. We spend our day working, necessarily preoccupied, our minds on what we are doing. When we return home, there is TV, conversation, activities and preoccupations of all kinds. Eventually we go to bed, where perhaps we read or watch a bit more TV. Finally we fall asleep.

When, in all of this, did we take time to think, to be contemplative, to pray, to wonder, to appreciate, simply to enjoy, to be restful, to be grateful just for being alive, to be grateful for love, for health, for God? The day just sucked us through.

I suspect that your coffee circles are similar to mine. Where I live, in the few contemplative moments that we take, we sit around talking: "It's a rat race. We should do something. We drive too hurriedly, we live too impatiently, we eat too fast, we work too hard, we are too preoccupied, too busy, we don't take time to smell the flowers!" But nothing changes.

As Mark Twain said: "It's like the weather—everyone complains about it, but nobody does anything about it."

Socrates commented that "the unexamined life is not worth living." I suspect that our age would counter with "the unlived life is also not worth examining." We have taken to examining our lives less and less.

The effect of this is the same everywhere. We see it in the way we eat, in the way we drive, in our inability to relax, in our lack of humor and reflectiveness and—need I say it—in our lack of prayer.

I do not want to be judgmental but I suspect that most persons in our culture pray very little, at least in terms of private prayer. I suspect that the average person's prayer life consists of a short hurried prayer in the morning, an even more distracted and hurried prayer before meals and another hurried prayer before retiring at night. That's precious little.

But our inability to be contemplative does not only show itself in our lack of private prayer. That is merely a symptom of something more deeply amiss. What our hurried lifestyle and our propensity for distraction is really doing is robbing us of solitude. As solitude diminishes, life seems less and less worth living.

Ironically most of us crave solitude. As our lives grow more pressured, as we grow more tired and as we begin to talk more about burnout, we fantasize about solitude. We imagine it as a peaceful, quiet place, ourselves walking by a lake, watching a peaceful sunset, smoking a pipe in a rocker by the fireplace. But even there we make solitude yet another activity, something we do. We attempt to take solitude like taking a shower. It is understood as something we stand under, endure, get washed by—and then return to normal life.

Solitude, however, is a form of awareness. It is a way of being present and perceptive within all of life. It is having a dimension of reflectiveness in our ordinary lives that brings with it a sense of gratitude, appreciation, peacefulness, enjoyment and prayer. It is the sense, within ordinary life, that ordinary life is precious, sacred and enough.

How do we develop such a dimension within our lives? How do we foster solitude? How do we get a handle on life so that it does not just suck us through? How do we begin to lay a foundation for prayer in our lives? How do we come to gratitude and appreciation within ordinary life?

Eric Fromm was asked to give a simple recipe for psychic health in a culture that is as pressured as ours.

"A half-hour of silence once a day, twice a day if you can afford the time. That will do marvels for your health," he answered.

Fromm's answer was not intended to be a religious one. He was no Thomas Merton. But it might have come from Merton. I can think of no better spiritual advice to give to a culture that conspires against interiority.

Try prayer and silence. One half an hour a day. Twice a day, if you can afford the time. It will do marvels for your health. As well, in a culture that conspires against the interior life, it will be a political act.

Praying Through a Crisis

WE ALL HAVE our moments of chaos and crisis. Loss, death, sickness, disappointment, hurt, loneliness, hatred, jealousy, obsession, fear; these come into our lives and often we find ourselves overwhelmed by the darkness they cause.

What can we do about them? How can we pull ourselves out of the dark chaos they put us into?

The simple answer of course is prayer. But that answer is given far too simplistically. We have all heard the phrases, so true in themselves: "Pray it through! Take your troubles to the chapel! Give it to God! God will help you!"

I can speak only for myself, though I suspect that my experience has its parallels in other lives, and I have found that often when I try to pray through some deep hurt I find no relief and, at times, end up more depressed, more immersed in the chaos, and more obsessively self-preoccupied than before praying.

Often I end up sucking the prayer into my own narcissism.

Too often when we try to pray when hurting, the prayer serves not to uproot the hurt and the narcissism, but to root it even more deeply in self-pity, self-preoccupation and darkness.

We end up further letting go of God's Spirit and, instead, giving in to panic, fear, chaos, non-forgiveness, obsession and resentment, in a word, to the posture of masturbation, of non-prayer.

Why? Is God not willing to help? Is it simply a question of patience? God will eventually help, but not yet?

God is always willing to help and, yes, we must be patient, healing takes time. But there is more involved. When we pray and our prayers do not help, then we are praying incorrectly. I have learned this painfully through years of mistakes.

Prayer is a focus upon God, not upon ourselves. When we are hurting or obsessed, the problem is that we are able to think about only one thing, the object of our hurt or loss. That concentration becomes depressive, oppressively focusing us so much upon one thing that we are unfree emotionally to think about or enjoy other things. Depression is an over-concentration.

For this reason, whenever we are caught up in depression, it is important that our prayer be completely focused upon God and not upon ourselves.

If we do what comes naturally when trying to "pray through a crisis" we will end up thinking about the crisis, wallowing in our own sufferings.

Instead of freeing ourselves from the sense of loss or obsession, we will pull the wound inward, make the pain worse and the depression even more paralyzing.

When we pray in a crisis we must force ourselves to focus upon God or Jesus or upon some aspect of their sacred mystery, and we must resist entirely the urge to relate that encounter immediately to our wounded experience.

Let me illustrate this with an example: Imagine yourself suffering the loss of someone you deeply loved. Hurt, unable to think about anything else, you go to pray. Immediately the temptation will be to focus upon your heart, your obsession. You will try to "talk it through," however sincerely. But the result will be disastrous. You will find yourself becoming more fixed upon what you are trying to free yourself from. Your depression will intensify.

Conversely if you force yourself, and this will be extremely difficult, to focus upon God—for example, as he reveals himself in some mystery of Christ's life—your depression will be broken. You will experience God, slowly but gently, widening again the scope of your heart and mind. With that will come an emotional loosening and freeing.

When a wounded child climbs into its mother's lap, it draws so much strength from the mother's presence that its own wound becomes insignificant. So too with us when we climb into the lap of our great Mother God. Our crisis soon domesticates and comes into a peaceful perspective, not because it goes away, but because the presence of God so overshadows us.

But this means we must genuinely climb into the lap of God. Like the wounded child we must be focused upon the mother, not upon ourselves. Concretely this means that, when praying in a crisis, we must refuse to think about ourselves at all, we must refuse even to relate the mystery we are meditating to ourselves and our wound. Like a child, we must simply be content to sit and be held by the mother.

That will be hard, very hard, to do. Initially every emotion in us will demand that we focus ourselves back upon our hurt. But that is the key, do not do it!

Do not, under the guise of prayer, wallow further in hurt. Rather focus upon God. Then, like a sobbing child at its mother's breast, in silence, we will drink that which nurtures and brings peace.

At the breast of God we drink the Holy Spirit, the milk of charity, joy, peace, patience, goodness, mildness, longsuffering, faith, chastity, hope and fidelity. In that nourishment lies peace.

Getting Angry with God

A LADY came to see me who was suffering from a curious resentment. She was angry at God. Her feelings were vague and not clearly focused, but she felt that somehow God was to blame for her unhappiness.

Life, she felt, was rapidly passing her by and she had already missed out on many chances for really living it. She was, and had been, a good lady, religious, moral, generous, living for others, faithful to her commitments.

Now in her mid-fifties she felt anger and resentment growing within her, an anger and resentment she was unable really to explain, accept or control.

She was confused and unhappy. On the one hand she did not regret her past life. She had been faithful, unselfish and religious. Yet, on the other, with her youth, health, sexual prowess, and opportunities fading, she felt frustrated, unneeded, unfulfilled, used, locked-in, and haunted by the thought that perhaps she had never made a decision for herself in her whole life.

Viewed one way, her virtue seemed like an accident, a conspiracy of circumstances. She wondered whether she had really chosen this or whether it had been forced upon her. Whenever she felt like that she filled with regret and resentment. She regretted that she had always been so moral, religious and proper. In these moments too she would have to admit to herself that she secretly envied the amoral, the unvirtuous, all those who never felt, as she did, the yoke of domestication that eventually comes with morality and religion.

At the root of all this was the feeling that she had been had, seduced by God. God was to blame. He, she assured me, had always been just real enough to hold her, but never real enough to fulfill her, at least not emotionally.

So she was angry, and angry with herself for being angry. She was full of resentment and full of guilt for being resentful. Prayer was difficult for her because she could not admit to herself that she was angry at God and so whenever she did try to pray it seemed artificial and contrived.

What does one say to a person like that? One begins by pointing out that her resentment and anger are already a high form of prayer, at least potentially so.

Too often we are under the impression that God does not want us to struggle with him, that he prefers sheep who docilely acquiesce (even as they swallow hard on the bitterness that so spontaneously arises in the emotional, psychological and sexual mechanisms which he built into them).

But God wants to be wrestled with. As Rabbi Heschel points out, ever since the days when Abraham argued with God over the fate of Sodom and Gomorrah, and Jacob wrestled with the angel, those close to God have also occasionally engaged in similar arguments.

The refusal to accept the harshness of God's ways in the name of his love is an authentic form of prayer. Indeed the prophets and saints were not always in the habit of simply saying "Thy will be done."

They often fought, challenged, squirmed and begged as a way of saying "Thy will be changed!" I suspect that they did sometimes annul divine plans. God wants to be struggled with, especially if we have been living in his house for a while.

Why? Why would he want this? How can wrestling be a form of prayer?

Wrestling can be a form of prayer precisely because it can be a form of love. People who live together in love for a long time must resolve many tensions. There is constant wrestling, much anger and occasional bitterness. But the struggling together, if persevered in, always leads to new depth in love.

The lady I was describing was in fact standing at the very edges of a new phase of love. She needed to pray through her bitterness first. As she stood at the edges of that new phase, bent under the weight of God's yoke, bitter and with the jealousy of Cain in her eyes, the same Father who had pleaded with the older brother of the prodigal son was also pleading with her, to enter a new circle, the circle of those who feel compassion for God.

Rabbi Heschel tells the story of a Polish Jew who became bitter and stopped praying "because of what happened in Auschwitz." Later, however, he began praying again. When asked "Why?" he replied, "I felt sorry for God."

This man had reached a new phase of love, that of affinity, of compassion. God's concerns, God's cause, God's house, were now his too. But such a point is only reached after struggle, when anger and bitterness are transformed.

God invites and I dare say enjoys the struggle. As Nikos Kazantzakis puts it:

Every person partakes of the divine nature in both spirit and flesh. The struggle between God and the human person breaks out in everyone, together with the longing for reconciliation. Most often this struggle is unconscious and short-lived. A weak soul does not have the endurance to resist the flesh for long. It grows heavy, becomes flesh itself, and the contest ends. The stronger the soul and the flesh, the more fruitful the struggle and the richer the final harmony. God does not love weak souls and flabby flesh. The Spirit wants to have to wrestle with flesh which is strong and full of resistance.

May we all win—by losing!

From Fantasy to Fulfillment

THERE IS something so nice about daydreaming. There, our dreams can come true and we attain that one-in-a-billion specialness that we ache for. In our daydreams we are the superstars: we write the songs, score the goals, dance the ballets and are so successful, beautiful, great and impressive that all our critics are silenced and all the persons we desire most fall in love with us.

It is no accident that we so often escape into the world of daydreams, because there we can live life without tears, without limits and without failure. In fantasy we achieve salvation, consummation and vindication.

We seldom admit to each other that we have daydreams and that we escape into them. We are ashamed of our fantasies, ashamed that, as adults, we resort to such a childish and egoistical escape. Imagine what others would think if they could tune into our fantasies!

But a certain escape into fantasy and daydreams is natural and even healthy. Daydreaming can be a way of relaxing.

There is little difference between a tired person inserting a musical cassette tape into a stereo and sitting back to forget life's problems and another tired soul inserting her favorite daydream into her imagination and sitting back to relax. Both can be a healthy escape from over-intensity and there should be no more shame in one than in the other.

Moreover a healthy fantasy life can positively help spawn creativity because our daydreams put us in touch with the goodness and potential that is inside us.

In our daydreams we are never small, petty persons but heroes and heroines, special persons who change worlds, radiate specialness, are truly creatures in God's image and likeness and are aesthetic and pedagogical incarnations of life's infinite potential. Nobody with a healthy fantasy life stagnates, because his daydreams make him too restless simply to vegetate.

However, daydreams can also be bad, not because we should be ashamed that, like children, we resort to fantasy, or because at times our imaginings are erotic and sexual, but because too great a reliance on fantasy fixates us. Simply put, if we daydream too much we become unhealthily self-preoccupied.

Too much fantasy dulls full attentiveness to the present, to others, to prayer and to God. Too much daydreaming leaves us distracted and dissipated with too much of our perception and thought centered upon our own agendas and our own obsessions. We become like a preoccupied and anxious man who takes a walk in a beautiful forest. Because his thoughts are obsessively fixed upon himself and his worries, he sees virtually nothing. All nature's beautiful colors, its multi-scents and million sounds are blocked out. He is lost in his own world, oblivious to the richness and beauty around him. He truly sees "as through a glass, darkly."

What should we do about our daydreams and our fantasy life?

To the extent that our daydreams are healthy, we may enjoy them. However, more and more, as we mature in life and prayer, we must actively work at turning away from fantasy toward prayer. How can we do this?

First we need to understand something about prayer. Prayer is more than just saying prayers. Radical prayer is contemplation, and contemplation itself should not be understood simply as good feelings we have when we gaze at something which moves us.

We contemplate every time we see something as it really is, nakedly, face to face.

When we genuinely perceive, when we see, hear, smell, touch or taste anything that is other than ourselves and do not manipulate it, we are contemplating, we are praying. (This of course does not preclude other methods of praying.)

When prayer is understood in this wide sense, then we see, too, how our daydreams can hurt us; namely, to the extent that when we daydream we focus our awareness ultimately upon ourselves, thereby limiting how much we see, hear, feel, touch and smell. Daydreaming gets in the way of prayer.

How concretely may we turn from daydreams to prayer?

You begin by avoiding the common misunderstanding that would identify contemplation with a blank state of mind.

We contemplate when we let our perception and thought form and flow freely without the manipulation that our preoccupations and obsessions normally impose. Contemplation is stream of awareness and stream of consciousness.

This is different from fantasy. When we daydream we actively manipulate our thoughts and imagination. In effect we play a program in our minds.

Contemplation is awareness without manipulation. Such awareness, as great spiritual writers have always assured us, is prayer.

It is enjoyable to daydream but it is ultimately more enriching to pray.

6

*

LIVING UNDER THE MERCY: GOD AND SCRAMBLED EGGS

The Christian is not the noble anti-hero
luxuriating in despair but the child of the
kindgom, the grace-merry person who blends
the perils of human freedom with the pursuing grace of God. She does not deny evil
but installs it in the movement of hope. In
her life, as in all life, there are tears and
laughter, but ultimately there is laughter,
the laughter of the resurrected Christ.

(JOHN SHEA)

God Overcomes Scrambled Eggs

SOME YEARS AGO a young man came to me for confession. It was a difficult confession for him. He had been having an affair with a girl and she had become pregnant. For a series of reasons marriage was out of the question. The pregnancy would, irrevocably, disrupt both their lives, not to mention the life of the child who would be born.

Being a sensitive person he needed no reminders that he had been irresponsible. He made no attempt to rationalize, to offer excuses or to escape blame. He recognized that he had sinned.

He also recognized that he had helped create a situation that was irrevocable, a certain ease and innocence had been destroyed, some things would never again be the same.

He ended his confession on a note of sadness and hopelessness: "There is no way I'll ever live normally again, beyond this. Even God can't unscramble an egg!"

What this young man was saying was that, for him, there would always be a skeleton in the closet. Ordinary life would, in its own way, limp along but he would remain forever marked by this mistake.

Today we live in a world and a church in which this kind of brokenness and attitude are becoming more the rule than the exception. For more and more people there is a major something to live beyond, some skeleton in the closet: a broken marriage, an abortion, a religous commitment that did not work out, a pregnancy outside marriage, a betrayed trust, a broken relationship, a soured affair, a serious mistake, a searing regret; sometimes with a sense of sin, sometimes without it.

Sadly for many, this comes, as it did for the young man, coupled with a hopelessness, a sense that something irrevocable has happened.

What we need today in the church, perhaps more than anything else, is a theology of brokenness which relates failure and sin seriously enough to redemption. Too often what is taught as redemption is little more than the strict law of karma: one chance per lifetime, salvation through getting it right, happiness and innocence only when there is nothing to be forgiven.

We have too much fear, in the end, of God. Ultimately we look at the scrambled egg, at our own mistakes and sins, and believe that the loss of a certain grace is irrevocable, that a mistake hangs us. Basically we do not believe that there is a second chance, let alone seventy-times-seven chances, that can be just as lifegiving as the first.

I was raised in a Catholicism which was deeply moral. It took commitment seriously and called sin sin. It was, on most moral issues, brutally uncompromising. It asked you not to betray, not to sin, not to make mistakes.

I have no regrets about that. In fact I feel pain for many today who are being raised in a moral relativism which excuses too much and challenges too little.

However, if the Catholicism that I was raised in had a fault, and it did, it was precisely that it did not allow for mistakes. It demanded that you get it right the first time. There was supposed to be no need for a second chance. If you made a mistake, you lived with it and, like the rich young man, were doomed to be sad, at least for the rest of your life. A serious mistake was a permanent stigmatization, a mark that you wore like Cain.

I have seen that mark in all kinds of people: divorcées, ex-priests, ex-religious, people who have had abortions, married people who have had affairs, people who have had children outside marriage, parents who have made serious mistakes with their children, and countless others who have made serious mistakes.

There is too little around to help them. We need a theology of brokenness.

We need a theology which teaches us that even though we cannot unscramble an egg God's grace lets us live happily and with renewed innocence far beyond any egg we may have scrambled.

We need a theology that teaches us that God does not just give us one chance, but that every time we close a door he opens another one for us.

We need a theology that challenges us not to make mistakes, that takes sin seriously, but which tells us that when we sin, when we make mistakes, we are given the chance to take our place among the broken, among those whose lives are not perfect, the loved sinners, those for whom Christ came.

We need a theology which tells us that a second, third, fourth and fifth chance are just as valid as the first one.

We need a theology that tells us that mistakes are not forever, that they are not even for a lifetime, that time and grace wash clean, that nothing is irrevocable.

Finally we need a theology which teaches us that God loves us as sinners and that the task of Christianity is not to teach us how to live, but to teach us how to live again, and again, and again.

Love Through Locked Doors

SEVERAL YEARS AGO a family I know well lost a daughter through suicide. She was in her late twenties and had become dangerously depressed. An initial attempt at suicide failed. The family then rushed round her. They brought her home, strove to be with her constantly, sent her to doctors and psychiatrists, and generally tried everything within their power to love and coax her out of her depression.

It did not work. Eventually, as I have said, she committed suicide.

Looking at her death and their efforts to love her and save her life, one sees how helpless at a certain point human love can be. Sometimes all the effort, patience and love in the world cannot get through to a frightened, sick, depressed person. In spite of everything, that person remains locked inside herself or himself, huddled against love, unfree, inaccessible, bent upon self-destruction.

No one who has ever dealt with a situation like this can have been immune to the deep feelings of discouragement, guilt, hopelessness and fear that ensue. Love, regardless of effort, seems powerless.

Fortunately we are not without hope and consolation. We believe in the ultimate redeeming power of love, and in the power of a love beyond our own that can do that redeeming. God's love is not stymied in the same way as ours. Unlike ours, it can go through locked doors, enter closed hearts and breathe peace and new life into frightened, paralyzed persons.

Our hope and our belief in this is expressed in one of the articles of our creed: "He descended into hell." What an incredible statement that is: God descended into hell. If that is true, and everything in Christ's life and teaching suggests that it is, then the very existence of an eternal hell is cast into doubt and the human heart has its ultimate consolation: Love will triumph.

We have not always understood those words however. Mostly we have taken them to mean that, between his death and resurrection, Jesus descended to some hell or limbo where lived the souls of all the good and just persons who had died since the time of Adam. Once there Jesus took them with him to heaven.

More recently various theologians have interpreted this article of the creed to mean that, in his death, Christ experienced alienation from his Father, and thus experienced in a real sense the pain of hell.

Irrespective of the merits of these interpretations, the doctrine of the descent into hell is first and foremost a doctrine about love. God's love for us, and the power of that love to go all lengths, to descend to all depths and to go through virtually every barrier in order to redeem a wounded, huddled, frightened, paranoid, alienated and unfree humanity.

By dying as he did, Christ shows that he loves us in such a way that he can descend into our private hells. His love is so empathetic and compassionate that it can penetrate all barriers that we construct out of hurt and fear and enter right into our despair and hopelessness.

We see this idea expressed powerfully in John 20. Twice

John presents the disciples as huddled behind closed doors, locked in because of fear. Twice John has Jesus come through the locked doors and stand in the midst of that frightened and depressed group and breathe peace into them.

That image of Christ going through locked doors is perhaps the most consoling within our entire faith. Put simply, it means that God can help us even when we cannot help ourselves. God can empower us even when we are too weak and despairing, even minimally, to open the door to let him in.

That is not only consoling, it is also corrective of a bad Pelagian spirituality that many of us were raised on.

I remember a holy picture that was given to me as a child. I saved it for years and its message has always haunted me in my darkest times. The picture shows a man, huddled and depressed in fear, in the dark behind a closed door. Outside stands Jesus with a lighted lantern, knocking softly on the door. The door has a knob only on the inside, the man's side. Jesus has no doorknob. He can only knock.

Beneath the picture, and everywhere in it by implication, is written: Only you can open that door! Salvation depends upon your effort.

That picture is not wholly without its merits, but ultimately what it says is untrue. Christ does not need a doorknob. Christ can enter closed doors. Christ can enter rooms and hearts that are locked out of fear.

The picture expresses a truth about human love. In the human arena, these are the dynamics of love; unless a heart opens from the inside, human love can only knock and it must remain outside.

But that is not the case with God's love, as John 20 depicts. God's love can descend into hell. Unlike our love, it is not left helplessly knocking at the door of fear, depression, hurt and sickness. It does not require that a person, especially a sick person, first finds the strength to make the initial move to open himself or herself to health.

In that lies ultimate consolation. There is no hell, no private hell of wound, depression, fear, sickness or even bitterness that God's love cannot and will not descend into. Once there, it will breathe out the peace of the Holy Spirit.

Suicide, Despair and Compassion

IT WAS a bad spring, not for weather but for suicides. Warm, restless winds had stirred both nature and the human spirit and for some it was more than they could handle.

Most of us have been raised to think of suicide as the ultimate despair, the final and unforgivable sin. A true suicide could be this, but almost all actual suicides have little to do with sin and despair.

Suicide, it was argued, was a refusal to hope, an irrevocable closing of oneself to forgiveness and new life. As G. K. Chesterton put it, suicide is the refusal to take an interest in existence; the refusal to take an oath of loyalty to life. A person who commits suicide, he contended, defiles every flower by refusing to live for its sake.

Chesterton would be correct if people did in fact commit suicide out of despair. Normally, they do not. The propensity for suicide is, in most cases, a psychological illness, a terminal disease which is no more sinful or indicative of despair than are cancer, high blood pressure and heart attacks.

We are creatures of body and soul—either can break down. Some die from physical cancer, high blood pressure or heart attacks. Others die from emotional cancer, high blood pressure and heart attacks. In both cases the death is not freely chosen. In both cases there is no despair.

Normally too we see Judas' death as the prototype of despair. Poor Judas! He betrayed Jesus and then was unable to accept forgiveness and so took a rope and hanged himself—and Jesus himself commented that it would be better for him if he had never been born.

To Judas we contrast Peter, who also betrayed Jesus. Peter, however, was able to accept forgiveness. Unlike Judas who despaired, Peter went out, had a good cry, accepted Christ's forgiveness and became the rock upon which the church was founded.

But such an interpretation, regardless of how deeply it is enshrined in Christian piety and popular tradition, is simplistic and, in the end, itself despairs of the compassion of God. The dynamics involved in accepting forgiveness and love are far more tied up with how much unconditional love we have been given than they are with virtue and faith.

If, when we are little children, those around us love us in such a way that we have a sense that we are lovable even when we make mistakes and if those around us give us the sense that love does not have to be earned or merited, then we will grow up to be persons who are able to accept forgiveness, as Peter did.

Perhaps the difference between Peter and Judas was not so much that Peter loved Jesus more, but that he had been given more unconditional love (as a free gift). Because of this he could accept forgiveness.

Looked at humanly, Judas despaired and Peter did not. I doubt whether such an assessment is correct. If it were, then love and eternal life would only be for the lucky and the strong. But God's compassion and understanding are not limited as ours are.

After the resurrection we see Christ, time and again, going through "closed doors" to breathe the spirit of peace and love upon huddled, frightened and miserable disciples. He still descends into hell, entering closed hearts, to breathe peace and love in places where there is huddling in fear and hurt.

Our ability for compassion and empathy and unconditional love is limited. When we meet certain barriers, we are helpless and can go no further. But God's compassion can go through closed doors and closed hearts. It descends into hell.

Most suicide victims are trapped persons, caught up in a private emotional hell which is an illness and not a sin. Their suicide is a desperate attempt to end unendurable pain, much like a man whose clothing has caught fire might throw himself through a window.

They are not, on the other side, met by our human judgments, but by a heart, a compassion, a love and a Mother whose understanding and tenderness is beyond our present imagination. She descends into their hell, holds them to her breast and breathes the spirit of peace and love over their fear and hurt.

Then finally they experience that unconditional love and tensionless peace which eluded them during their lives on earth.

The Cross as Unconditional Love

THE CROSS OF CHRIST is like a well-cut diamond. Turn it in the sun and you get a variety of colors and sparkles. Among other things, it brings out the price of true love, the power of vulnerability to bring about community, the presence of God within human suffering, how death washes things clean, how death can be triumph, how one is tempted to cry out in despair just before triumph, and especially how God loves us unconditionally.

The unconditional love of God is what Good Friday is, in the end, all about. That is why it is called Good Friday, not Black Friday.

This was brought home to me, powerfully, several years ago. A man in his mid-thirties came to see me. He did not ask for confession, but he made one.

He sat himself down and said simply, "Father, I want to tell you a story. The worst thing that could possibly happen to anyone has happened to me—and the best thing that could ever happen to anyone has also happened to me. I have been to hell and back—and being in hell led me to believe in heaven."

Tears flowed freely as he told me his story. He was a married man with three children. His marriage was basically a good one, though he had been unfaithful. Unthinking, without prayer in his life, seduced by his own selfishness and the pressures of our culture, he had drifted into a sexual affair with one of the secretaries in his office. Initially he experienced very little guilt about the affair and continued on with his family, the church, and his work as before.

"It was incredible," he confessed, "but I was able to continue this with basically no guilt feeling whatever. In fact I even believed that this was helping the girl involved and was making me a better husband and father."

Eventually the girl became pregnant. Even then his irresponsibility did not sink in. He continued as before. She did not.

Returning from a holiday with his family he found a letter waiting for him. The girl had written to tell him that she had had an abortion, had quit her job, and had moved to another town. It was over. It was then that the reality of his sin sunk in, deeply and painfully. Before that moment he had felt little guilt. Now, in an instant, he was overwhelmed by it. His world shattered. Guilt overcame him and, unable to see how he would ever again face God, his family, and himself, he decided, though in a vague sort of way, to kill himself. With no particular plan in mind, he sat in his car on the night on which he had received the letter, and began to drive.

Eventually, after some hours, he found himself on unmade roads and finally, not knowing where he was, he ran out of gasoline. Leaving the car, he saw an old dilapidated church. Its doors were torn off their hinges and he walked blindly in and fell asleep. He awoke just as the sun was rising. When he looked around he saw that the only thing left in the church was a crucifix on the front wall.

He said, "You know, Father, I'm a cradle Catholic. I've seen crucifixes all my life. But, before that moment, I had never really seen one. I looked at that cross and I understood. I had been to hell and God has never stopped loving me, even for one second!"

Then he added, "I'm not proud of what I did. That sin will always be part of my past, nothing will ever erase that. But because of what I experienced in seeing that cross and knowing what it means, I can live beyond that. I know now that God loves me even when I am twisted and sinful. From that, I draw strength to live new, beyond my sin."

Reflecting upon that story, I was reminded of a comment theologian Jürgen Moltmann made about the cross of Christ:

> The cross is the utterly incommensurable factor in the revelation of God. We have become far too used to it. We have surrounded the scandal of the cross with roses. We have made a theory of salvation out of it. But that is not the cross . . . On the cross, God is non-God. Here is the triumph of death, the enemy, the non-church, the lawless state, the blasphemer, the soldiers. Here Satan triumphs over God. Our faith begins at the point where atheists suppose that it must be at an end. Our faith begins with the bleakness and power which is the night of the cross, abandonment, temptation and doubt about everything that exists! Our faith must be born where it is abandoned by all tangible reality; it must be born of nothingness, it must taste this nothingness and be given it to taste in a way that no philosophy of nihilism can imagine. (*The Crucified God*, n.e. 1976)

Our faith begins where we would think it ends. The darkness of hell, the blackness of Good Friday, perhaps more so than anything else, can help us understand the love that makes for heaven.

It is this love that we celebrate when we celebrate Christ's death.

The love that emanates from the cross of Jesus is not something to be admired, adored, but is to be seized and lived under.

Living Under a Merciful God

IN THE PAST FEW YEARS, both teaching and writing, I have frequently been challenged by persons who feel that I am going soft on part of the Christian message. There are a number of variations to the critique, but generally it sounds like this:

"You make it too easy! You sound as if it is easy to go to heaven. You talk as if there was no hell, or, at least, as if very few persons end up there. Doesn't Scripture itself say that the road that leads to life is narrow—and few find it! Aren't you leading people astray by giving them the impression that almost everyone is going to heaven?"

Not infrequently too I have been quoted the visions of a certain mystic who saw souls going to hell like snowflakes.

What to make of all of this? Is it true that the majority of people are going to hell while a minority are being saved?

Is it true that there is somewhere, however it is conceived of, a great book, a law of karmic justice, within which all is noted and all will have to be accounted for?

Underneath this fear of making heaven too easy there generally lies a sound instinct. Like Jesus, it affirms that the choices we make in this life are serious; that sin is important and real; that the passage to life, life in the here and now, is not easily found (as we can attest from experience—who really is happy?). We can lose heaven. Hell is a real option.

What is less sound in this insistence upon the narrow road and the importance of preaching the dangers of hell is the vision of God that undergirds it. In the end, any vision that sees souls going into hell like snowflakes is not one that takes seriously the God that Jesus talked about.

To affirm that the majority of persons are being lost in terms of eternity denies the unconditional love of God and the power of that love ultimately to redeem sin and woundedness.

Simply put, the love of the God that Jesus called his and our Father would not tolerate a situation within which the millions are going to an eternal hell, like snowflakes, while a mere few are finding the narrow way. This God would redo the incarnation, not to mention creation itself.

Christ's coming to save us is not so much a story of some mysterious drama that God deemed necessary to be played out so that some alienation caused by our first parents could be overcome. No. The drama of the incarnation has as its central point the revelation of the heart of God, a heart of infinite love which can, even given human sin, bring about the salvation of most, perhaps all persons.

What does this mean?

First of all it means that God loves us unconditionally and that there is nothing we can do, sin included, that even for one second can change that. God is present to us, loving us, even in our twistedness and perversity. We can go to hell and, even there, God does not stop loving us. That is in fact the meaning of the phrase "he descended into hell." We are loved unconditionally and for ever, even in our sin.

Hence we live under the law of mercy, not of justice. There is no great book, or great law, within which all sins are recorded and where a pound of retribution is demanded for a pound of sin. Sin need not be undone, nor even atoned for, by humans. It can be freely forgiven, washed clean without retribution because of Christ's sacrifice.

It is interesting to note that among the great religions of the world only Christianity, Judaism and Islam do not believe in reincarnation. Why? Because they all believe in the same God, a God who does not demand retribution but can make everything clean with one embrace. There is no need to keep reliving life until one gets it right.

We are loved unconditionally and for ever. Salvation, going to heaven, is nothing other than accepting this.

Of course we can, and in this life we often do, reject this. That is why here, in this life, most of us have not yet found the road that leads to life. Few of us are really happy, actually redeemed by love.

It is easy to go to hell in this life. It is not so easy, however, to stay there for eternity. Why? Because here, in this life, most often nobody can descend into our private hell—our woundedness, our fundamental alienation, our sin, our paranoia, our fantasy and our fear—and breathe out there unconditional love, understanding and acceptance. Hence in this life we are often in hell, miserable, biting so as not to be bitten, sinning so as to compensate for being outside love.

However, God's love can, as we see in Christ's death and resurrection, descend into hell and embrace and bring to peace tortured and paranoid hearts.

Our moral choices in this life are crucial. We can, and frequently do, make choices that make it harder for us to accept unconditional love. Moreover there is a real danger of not sinning honestly, of rationalizing and of warping ourselves so that a permanent hell becomes a real possibility.

But this is, I submit, rare. Few people when confronted by an unconditional embrace will resist. That is why most people will go to heaven.

In saying that, I am not going soft on the Christian message. I am, I believe, affirming the greatest truth there is.

The Cross Symbolizes Hope for All

THE PASSION AND DEATH of Christ is a timeless mystery, throwing redemption backward and forward in time. It is timeless, too, in that it is ongoing. It is still being lived out. Christ is still dying, in multifarious fashion, within our sufferings. We all have our passion narratives, our Good Friday stories at whose center lies the cross, with all its bitter shame and real death.

Recently a lady shared with me her passion narrative. With her permission I share it with you, verbatim, uncensored, earthy, tragic. It is the passion of our Lord Jesus Christ according to one of millions of contemporary evangelists, God's poor, who in their bodies and hearts taste the gall of Good Friday:

> When people look at me all they see is my anger. I guess I am an angry person since I don't have a whole lot of friends right now. Everyone likes bouncy people . . . with their big smiles and their bouncy personalities. I lost my bounce years ago. It's taken me all these years to really understand why.
>
> Father, you should read this book. It's Mary Gordon's *Temporary Shelter*. In it she has an essay on violation. I wish I had read it twenty-five years ago. The years of frustration it might have saved me. She tells her story, how she was, twice, raped—once by her

own uncle. Funny, how hearing someone else's story doesn't make your own sound so bad.

Well, my story is bad. Sexually abused by my own dad at nine. Something inside of me died then. It's forty years later and, really, I'm still in shock. My whole life really ended then. I remember reading a book by Joyce Carol Oates, and she simply said: "and the spirit went out of the man!" That's what happened to me . . . the spirit left me at nine. I've had no enthusiasm, really, for life ever since.

I went through some times when I was able to bury it, to leave it behind, to pretend, to go on with life, to act normal, like everyone else. Yeah, I went through the motions—I fell in love (kind of), I got married, had three kids—and for a while I even thought it was behind me. I was even able to forgive my dad (kind of). I remember coming home for his funeral, seeing him there in his coffin in the funeral home. His face looked peaceful (more peaceful than I'd ever remembered him in life). The tension and anger that were always there seemed to have drained away with his life. He looked peaceful. I kissed him. I made my peace. He was dead and I wanted to let him and it go! But it didn't die. It didn't go.

It started with my reading feminist books, but I know that it would have come out anyways, in a different way. I read those books and it put me in touch with my wound. I understood a lot. And I got angrier: if only, if only . . . if only my father hadn't been so sick, if only society was fairer, if only women had equal rights and power, if only men weren't so damn macho! If only . . . Well, I got angrier and angrier. I froze up inside like an iceberg. I was hardest on my family—my husband, my kids, and then on those around me, the parish, my friends, everyone! God, I fought—and I was right too! It is unfair. It is a damned shame that lives, especially women's lives, can be forever ruined so easily. It is unfair to live in a world that isn't fair to us.

Yeah, my anger ruined my marriage, it ruined my relationship to a church I once loved and respected; it ruined my happiness. But something else ruined me long before that! I wish somebody understood that.

Sometimes I think that's true, even of God! I've grown tired of praying. For a while I was taken with the idea of God as woman. But, in the end, God, father or mother, who gives a damn?

I've such mixed feelings. Sometimes, I don't even want ever to be healed or happy. I just want to cling, cling like hell to this god-awful death that wasn't my fault, that isn't fair!

But something else inside me wants to let go. I want some life back, some joy back, some love back. I wasn't born this angry, I don't want to die this angry! I don't want to be this angry!

Funny how through all this, the anger, the bitterness, my leaving the church and all, what's come through to me is the cross. I don't know how to explain it, even to myself, but somehow that symbol gives me the hope that, somewhere, somebody does understand.

7

TOUCHING THE HEM OF THE GARMENT: RECONCILIATION AND EUCHARIST

A man who was entirely careless of spiritual things died and went to hell. And he was much missed on earth by his old friends. His business agent went down to the gates of hell to see if there was any chance of bringing him back. But, though he pleaded for the gates to be opened, the iron bars never yielded.

His priest went also and argued: "He was not really a bad fellow, let him out, please!"

The gates remained stubbornly shut against all their voices.

Finally his mother came, she did not beg for his release. Quietly, and with a strange catch in her voice, she said to Satan, "*Let me in.*" Immediately the great doors swung open upon their hinges. For love goes down through the gates of hell and there redeems the damned.

(Based upon thoughts by
G. K. CHESTERTON)

Incarnation Imparts Power

THERE IS A PAIN among us as Christians today that is too seldom talked about. It is the pain of losing a loved one, not through death or even through physical separation, but through the loss of a shared common faith, religious practice and morality.

Let me explain with an example: You are a parent trying to live out your Christian life in a conscientious fashion. You go to church regularly, pray, and basically live a decent moral life. When they were young, your children naturally followed you and shared your convictions and practice. Then gradually, or perhaps suddenly, they stopped going to church, stopped sharing your views on sexuality and marriage, and defiantly or apologetically began to live in a way that contradicts what you believe and practice.

At first you challenged and fought. You demanded that they went to church and lived as Christians sexually, but to no avail. Eventually, in frustration, you arrived at an unhappy truce: you continued to practice, they did not.

As a priest I have met literally dozens of parents (in half a dozen countries) who are anxious with worry about their children in this state. However this is not limited to parents worrying about children. This pain affects us all deeply. None of us has not felt the deep pain of loss when a son or daughter, a friend, or a brother or sister who used to walk beside us, no longer does.

One of the deepest bondings of all is weakened and

strained. We are pained: both because we feel a sense of loss and personal rejection and because we are worried about the other's long-term happiness and salvation as well as their long-term bonding with us.

This pain is very common, very deep, and too seldom talked about. How should we react? What can we do as parents, friends, brothers and sisters? What can we do as the body of Christ?

Obviously we can pray and continue to live out our own lives according to our own deepest convictions, hoping to love and challenge with our lives more than with our words. This is what we must do—and, most times, all we can do.

But it is important to understand what we are really doing when we are doing this. Something deeper is happening than is seen on the surface. What?

In John 20:23 Jesus tells the earliest Christian community: "Whose sins you forgive they are forgiven; whose sins you retain, they are retained." In Matthew 16:19 he tells Peter: "Whatever you bind on earth shall be considered bound in heaven; whatever you loose on earth shall be considered loosed in heaven."

The traditional interpretation of these texts takes their meaning to refer to the institution of the sacrament of reconciliation and to the giving of papal powers to Peter and his successors. They mean at least that much, but much more is implied. What Jesus is doing here is giving the *whole Christian community* the power to forgive sins and the power of binding and loosing. What does this mean concretely?

It means that if we are truly members of Christ's body then when we forgive sins, the person is forgiven. Likewise it means that if we love someone and hold them in our life, that person, regardless of his or her own actions, is not cut off from the body of Christ. If you continue to love somebody, they are bound.

Hell is only possible when one has put oneself totally outside of the range of love and forgiveness of the Christian community, when one has rendered oneself incapable of being loved and forgiven in that she or he has actively rejected not only the religious and moral convictions of the Christian community, but, more important, their love.

To make this concrete: If a child, or brother or sister or a loved one of yours strays from the church in terms of practice and morality, as long as you continue to love them, hold them in union and forgive them, they are bound, still part of the church (because of your love).

Irrespective of their official external relationship to the church and Christian morality they are in grace because you are part of the body of Christ and when someone touches you they are healed and forgiven, just as persons at the time of Jesus were healed by touching him.

When you love someone, unless they actively reject that love, they are bound—bound to the body of Christ, sustained in salvation.

And this is true even beyond death. If someone close to you dies in a state when, externally at least, he or she is not practicing as a Christian and is at odds morally with the body of Christ, your love and forgiveness will continue to bind them to the body and will continue to forgive them— even after death.

Soft-Pedaling the Truth?

SEVERAL YEARS AGO, following a talk I had given, I was asked a series of questions about morality, sin, confession and forgiveness. I began my response with a few distinctions calculated to show how complex these questions were and was moving on to the next step, an attempt to give some answers, when a man present lost his patience and his temper.

He challenged me angrily, "Father, why are you fudging around in answering this? You know the answer, every Catholic does! Sex outside of marriage, missing mass on Sundays, these are mortal sins, and no theological or psychological distinctions can change that! You know too, only too well, that the Catholic Church teaches clearly, and has defined at the Council of Trent, that there is only one way to have serious sin forgiven, confession to a priest. Not to say that clearly is to soft-pedal the truth!"

I was searching for a response when a lady stood up, shaking and nearly overcome with emotion, and spoke for me.

"This is not soft-pedaling the truth. I believe what Father is saying . . . and I'll tell you why. I had a nineteen-year-old daughter who was killed in a car accident two years ago. She hadn't been going to church for over a year before that and she was living with her boyfriend. But she was a good girl, with a good heart, and nobody is going to tell me that she went to hell!"

More recently, at a diocesan conference on the sacrament

of reconciliation, I had been explaining how reconciliation, like all sacraments, was a touching of the body of Christ and how, consequently, one could have one's sins forgiven through touching Christ's body within Christian community and within Eucharist. I went on to say that I considered the practice of confession a beautiful and important sacrament, one used by the mature, and the fact that many Christians today no longer practiced it was a bad sign. But that, despite the value and importance of private confession, radically we can and do have our sins forgiven through living and worshipping within Christian community and especially through receiving the Eucharist.

Again I was accused of soft-pedaling the truth. The Catholic tradition, I was passionately informed, is that all serious sin can only be forgiven through explicit confession to a priest.

I have been around long enough to know that this statement is generally perceived in fact as the Catholic tradition on reconciliation, and so I have had to think long and hard: am I soft-pedaling the truth? Does not the Council of Trent clearly demand private confession as the condition for the forgiveness of serious sin? Is a certain theology of the incarnation (upon which I base the belief that when one goes to Eucharist or participates otherwise in Christian community one is touching the hem of Christ's garment and is thus being reconciled) faulty? Am I being influenced by some liberal consensus which, blind to all except its own ideological concerns, is trying to be a surrogate for truth?

These are valid questions all religious teachers who know Christ's warning about scandalizing little ones had better ask themselves fairly regularly. There are penalties for playing loose with the truth.

But there are also dangers the other way, one can danger-ously reduce truth. One can also soft-pedal the incarnation. Just as one can lack the courage to affirm hard truths be-cause they demand things which go against the grain, one can easily lack the courage to affirm how incredible and far-reaching are the tentacles of the incarnation and how lavish the mercy of God that is revealed in it.

I doubt that any Christian who takes seriously what Jesus taught us about God would want to challenge the lady who claimed that, despite her daughter's wanderings and her dy-ing without explicit confession she was surely not in hell.

So what do courage and truth demand that we say? That there is no forgiveness for serious sin outside the explicit sacrament of reconciliation; or that Christian community and the Eucharist are the body of Christ on earth and that when we touch them with even a modicum of sincerity we are healed? That we take Trent's statement on private con-fession to mean that, outside explicit private confession, there can be, for any Catholic, no other means of reconcilia-tion; that we take the statement in its proper context and with all its qualifications and affirm, in the name of Trent, that there are ways outside explicit confession to have sins forgiven?

Do courage and truth demand that we teach that only Jesus can forgive sin and that, today, that forgiveness is dis-pensed only through private confession; or that we affirm, as does Scripture, that we do not replace the body of Christ, that we are not like his body, nor even that we are his mysti-cal body, but that we are his body, flesh, blood, tangible, in history, the ongoing incarnation, and consequently that when we forgive, Christ forgives; when we bind, Christ binds; when we console, Christ consoles; and when that woman loved and forgave her wandering daughter, Christ loved and forgave that wandering daughter?

In what does the greater danger lie—in soft-pedaling confession or in soft-pedaling and reducing the incredible love and forgiveness that are revealed in the incarnation?

Falling into God's Arms

WE LIVE IN too much fear of God, trusting too little that he understands and accepts us as we are, with all our adolescent mistakes, betrayals and weaknesses.

As an illustration, I offer you a rather poignant incident I was associated with some time back. I was officiating at the funeral of a man in his early twenties who was killed, while drunk, in a motor accident.

Death because of irresponsibility and drunkenness! Moreover during the last few years of his life he had been away from the church and the sacraments and had been living with his girl friend. This is hardly what classical spirituality calls "a happy death."

This young man had come from a good and faith-filled family who, despite the fact that his last years were filled with turbulence and immaturity, loved him very deeply.

Looking at faces at that funeral, it was evident that there was more than sorrow in them. Fear was present, real fear that this young man we had all known, loved, understood, and knew to have had a good heart, was somehow going to be excluded from heaven and condemned to hell because, for a few brief years of adolescence, he had been mixed up and somewhat irresponsible.

Strange and sad that we should be worried that God did not understand. We, with our limited minds and limited hearts, understood. We, with the fogginess that clouds our understanding, knew that, beneath it all, despite the circumstance of his life and death, he had a good heart, a warm heart, a loving heart that needed just a bit more time and love to burst into charity, chastity and faith. Strange that we should feel that God did not recognize this.

We knew how good this young man's heart was. We knew too that his irresponsibility was little more than a combination of adolescent immaturity, laziness, peer pressure and the infectious influence of an amoral culture. Deep down he was not bad, immoral, a candidate for condemnation. He was little more than a child, struggling, feeling his oats, showing off, insecure, merely looking for acceptance and love.

On that basis, can we seriously think that he might be excluded from the community of life? How utterly absurd!

A child in this state needs, perhaps, a spanking, a challenge, a shock, but that is light years from hellfire.

I knew this young man's parents. Because they were good Christians they were deeply hurt by his immaturities, his straying from the church and his disregard for the teachings on sexuality. The last years of his life and especially his death made a deep wound.

Yet, standing at his graveside, if they could have reached him, even for one second, there would have been no scolding, no bitterness, no demand for an explanation and apology. They would have wrapped their arms around him as they would a wounded child and conveyed to him in a language deeper than words that they understood.

Like the father of the prodigal son, they would not demand nor want any atonement before they would let go of their own hurt. They would simply be overwhelmed in the joy that they again had their son.

God is a God of infinite compassion. Even more than this young man's parents, God understood the goodness of this young man's heart.

I am sure God greeted him with an embrace that was as accepting and healing as the embrace of the father for the prodigal son.

I suspect that the only thing condemned that day was another fatted calf—for the feast!

The purpose of this is not to dwell on a particular example, but to challenge us to believe more deeply that God understands. Crassly put, God is not stupid!

If we, with our limits, can see beyond wound and struggle to a goodness that lies still deeper within a human heart, how much more does God see our goodness, understand our struggles and forgive our weaknesses. If we could believe this, then we would let God walk with us through all the patches of our lives, however dark and perverse. Not believing it leads us to the worst religious mistake of all: we run away from God whenever we need him the most.

It is precisely at those times when we have fallen, when we are morally impotent, bankrupt, struggling, and stand, unclean, with our sin on our hands, that we most, like a wounded child, need the embrace of a mother or father.

Unfortunately, too often that is precisely when we quit praying, quit going to church, quit receiving the sacraments and quit putting ourselves in God's arms. Why?

Because we feel we must first, by our own efforts, clean our house a bit and get our lives in order before we can approach God's arms; as if to approach God first requires a basic moral minimum. First clean the house, then call in the cleaners!

The Eucharist Is an Embrace

THERE IS A STORY told about a four-year-old Jewish boy, Mortakai, who refused to go to school to study Hebrew and the Torah. Every time his parents attempted to send him to school young Mortakai would sneak off to the swings and play by himself. His parents tried every form of persuasion and threat, but nothing worked. The child failed to understand or acquiesce, silently and stubbornly refusing to stay in school. Eventually they took him to see a psychiatrist. That too proved futile. He continued to sneak away from school at every opportunity.

Finally, in desperation, they took him to the rabbi, an old and spiritually astute man. The rabbi listened while the parents explained the problem. Without a word, he picked up the child and held him closely to his heart for several moments. Then, still without a word, he put the child down. From then on, Mortakai stayed in school and there was no further problem.

What do we do when our words are inadequate? What do we do when we feel tense and tired? What do we do when we feel inadequate to cope with the complexities and ambiguities of our lives and loves? What do we do when we need power from beyond ourselves to bring about a love, a wholeness and a peace, which we cannot give ourselves?

We generally do all kinds of things, not the least of which is that we often grow depressed, frustrated and despairing.

But there is something we can do. We can touch the hem

of Christ's garment. We can celebrate the Eucharist. In it we are inexplicably given peace and strength because in that ritual God holds us to his heart.

The scriptural story of the woman who touched the hem of Christ's garment provides a paradigm for this. That woman, we are told, had been suffering from internal bleeding for many years. During those years she had tried everything within her power to come to healing. Nothing had worked. All her efforts had served only to worsen her state and leave her fatigued and discouraged. Finally, with her own resources spent and all that was humanly in view exhausted, she decided she would sneak up and touch Christ. As she touched him she felt a power flow into her. She became whole.

Something from beyond herself, something from beyond ordinary possibility, now flowed where formerly she hemorrhaged. Her explicit confrontation with Christ would come later.

The Eucharist is meant to function like that. In it we touch the hem of Christ's garment and are held to his heart. What happens there is something beyond words and understanding, though not beyond love.

Like love, the Eucharist does not need to be understood or explained, it needs only to be touched. In the Eucharist, as in love, the main thing is that we are held.

Perhaps the most useful image of how the Eucharist functions is the image of a mother holding a frightened, tired and tense child. In the Eucharist God functions as a mother. God picks us up; frightened, tired, helpless, complaining, discouraged and protesting children, and holds us to her heart until the tension subsides and peace and strength flow into us.

A tense and tired child held to its mother's breast eventually becomes calm and returns to the floor again full of the mother's strength. Through an embrace the mother can im-

part to a child a peace and a strength that cannot be trans-
mitted through words. This is also true for the embrace of
friends and lovers.

There is in an embrace something beyond what can be
explained biologically or psychologically. Power is transmit-
ted through love that goes beyond rational understanding.

That is why after Jesus had spent all his words he left us
the Eucharist.

That is why after we have spent all our words we should
celebrate the Eucharist. When our own words, decisions and
actions are inadequate to relieve the aching in our hearts we
need the embrace of the mother, God. This happens in the
Eucharist.

It is a timeless ritual, an embrace. Like love, it is something that we can never fully understand or explain. But we
need not understand it. We can let the ritual do its work.
Ultimately we go to the Eucharist to let ourselves be held.

We live constantly at the limits of our own capacities,
where our words fail us, where our resources are not enough
and we feel acutely our dullness, our failure, our moral im-
potence, our bitterness and our distance from God and
others.

We are constantly helpless, helpless to heal and helpless
to celebrate. In that fatigue and tension we need to abandon
ourselves to the embrace, the Eucharist.

It is not important to understand all that transpires there,
nor even that we should go to the Eucharist fully alert and
enthusiastic—I doubt whether the apostles were that at the
Last Supper. It is only important that we enter the ritual. In it
God holds us to her heart.

Celebrating Our Alphabet

PERHAPS the most frequent complaint one hears in church circles is that our liturgical gatherings are so uninspiring and boring. Usually the celebrant, the priest, is singled out as the culprit and is asked to bear the brunt of the criticism. He is accused of being dead, uninspiring, bland, a poor preacher and downright boring.

As a priest I take more than a casual offense to this critique. It is not that I deny its truth. Heaven knows, most of the time our celebrations are dull, uninspiring and boring. It is no wonder that people see church attendance as a grim duty rather than a privilege.

But the fault, when there is one, is not solely ours as priests. In fact there is often no fault save the unrealistic expectations of those attending.

Are liturgical gatherings meant always to be exciting, bouncy, enthusiastic celebrations? Is the celebrant solely, or even primarily, responsible for making the celebration enthusiastic and exciting?

The answers to those questions are not so obvious. First, not all liturgical gatherings can, nor should, be enthusiastic, bouncy, high celebrations. Good liturgy is good psychology. It flows with the psychological rhythms of those attending. As well, good prayer, in the classical definition, means "lifting mind and heart to God."

Given that, the issue grows suddenly very complex. Our psyches go up and down. We have our seasons and days of enthusiasm, bounce, joyfulness. Sometimes we feel like singing and dancing. Sometimes there is spring in our step.

But we have other seasons too, cold seasons, bland seasons, seasons of tiredness, pain, illness, boredom. We try to get one foot in front of the next. If prayer is lifting heart and mind to God then clearly during those times we should be lifting something other than song and dance.

We gather in liturgical celebration to be challenged by God's word and to be nourished by his body, both as it is incarnate in the community and as it is in the Eucharist.

But we bring something too. The celebrant's role is not that of dictating what is to be lifted up to God. His role is to help gather it together and to direct it upward, as an incense smoke to God.

Thus the best celebrant is not necessarily the one who conducts the most bouncy and enthusiastic celebration, nor even the one who delivers the best homily. Sometimes the celebrant's very efforts to do this can do violence to the persons attending.

It can mean a lack of respect, not to mention a secondary and superficial understanding of what is meant by redemptive joy, to tell an overtired, over-extended, emotionally wounded and bored person that he or she is not celebrating properly because they are not responding with vigorous enthusiasm.

The best celebrant is the person who can act as a radar screen, the one who can lift up not just the bread and wine, but all that the folks bring—including their tiredness, their hangovers, their woundedness, their emotional and sexual preoccupations, and their boredom.

In the end a celebrant is limited, sometimes severely, by what the people themselves bring to the celebration.

Who is he celebrating for? The happy? The tired? The

bouncy? The uptight? The bored? The hungover? The restless? The prayerfully attentive? The emotionally preoccupied? Whose heart and mind is he supposed to be lifting up
to God?

He must, I submit, gather it all together. He must offer it
as it is, and not as he would like it to be.

When we attend a liturgy we should be told: "Come as
you are! Pray as you are! Tell it as it is! Lift up your heart
and mind, not somebody else's. Celebrate it all, your joys,
your despairs, your woundedness, your tiredness, your boredom."

There is a story told about a Jewish farmer who, through
carelessness, did not get home before sunset one Sabbath and
was forced to spend the day in the field, waiting for sunset
the next day before being able to return home.

Upon his return home he was met by a rather perturbed
rabbi who chided him for his carelessness. Finally the rabbi
asked him: "What did you do out there all day in the field?
Did you at least pray?"

The farmer answered: "Rabbi, I am not a clever man. I
don't know how to pray properly. What I did was simply to
recite the alphabet all day and let God form the words for
himself."

When we come to celebrate we bring the alphabet of our
lives. If our hearts and minds are full of warmth, love, enthusiasm, song and dance, then these are the letters we bring.

If they are full of tiredness, despair, blandness, pain and
boredom, then those are our letters. Bring them. Spend them.
Celebrate them. Offer them. It is God's task to make the
words!

Worshipping in Anguish

FREQUENTLY THE COMPLAINT is made that our Christian gatherings, especially our Eucharists, are boring and devoid of a vital connection to life. Immediately the temptation is to respond by attempting to make our Eucharists more lively, more interesting, more full of song, more joyous. This, I submit, just as frequently compounds the issue as solves it. However good these things are in themselves, the root of the complaint is that, good singing and better homilies notwithstanding, in the end real life remains untouched.

Why?

Langdon Gilkey commented that the task of Christian worship is not to celebrate the God of special religious places, but the God of ordinary places. This is equally true regarding ourselves. Worship must not just celebrate the heart that people feel they should bring to religious places, but the heart as it beats in ordinary places.

Ordinary places contain some joy and some gratitude, but they are also filled with bitterness, suspicions, pettiness, paranoia, jealousy and more than enough heaviness.

We come together from ordinary places with these things partially paralyzing the joys of our hearts and, as we sit listening to the word and gather round the altar, these things do not automatically disappear. Our Eucharists, like our homes and places of work, are filled with suspicions, jealousies, judgments, paranoia and misunderstandings. We stand around the Eucharistic table with the same wounds we bring to our other tables.

Worship, then, is meant not just to celebrate our joys and gratitudes; its task is also to break us open, to make us groan in anguish, to lay bare our paranoia and to lessen the jealousies and the distance that sit between us. Here we are asked to be vulnerable before each other, to forgive and embrace each other. Bitterness, hatred and suspicion are supposed to disappear; and liturgy is supposed to help that happen.

It is on this point that our Eucharists are most anemic.

What is wrong generally is not that people do not sing and dance, but that they do not break down. There is too little anguish in our Eucharists.

To become one heart with each other involves anguish, the painful letting go of paranoia, selfishness, bitterness, hurt, jealousies, pettiness, narrowness of vision, aggressiveness, shyness and all those other things that keep us apart.

If our Eucharists do not succeed in breaking down the barriers that separate us from each other, then we can never hope to succeed in breaking down these same barriers in the world. As Jim Wallis put it: "In worship, the community is edified . . . if it does not edify itself here, it certainly will not do so in daily life, nor in the execution of its ministry to the world."

Christ was effective because Christ was vulnerable. He was also often in anguish.

It is interesting that the only ritual that Christ asks us to repeat over and over again is the Eucharist. In it we remember him as broken, poured out, empty, heartbroken, frightened, humiliated, vulnerable, in anguish. To celebrate this ritual properly we need to have in our hearts what

Christ had in his at the first Eucharist. What was he feeling then?

Joy and thanksgiving. Yes. Love for those at the table with him. Surely. But beyond this, his heart felt anguish, deep longing and fear at the prospect of the pain that was now a certainty before intimacy and community could be achieved.

It would perhaps do all of us good occasionally when we leave the Eucharist, instead of going to a lively meal with the folks, to go off as Jesus did after the first Eucharist, to a lonely place to have an agony in the garden and to sweat some blood as we ask for the strength to drink from the real chalice—the chalice of vulnerability.

Occasionally when St. Augustine handed the Eucharist to a communicant, instead of saying, "the body of Christ," he would say: *"Receive what you are."*

Augustine had perceived, for whatever reasons, that the words of consecration "this is my body, this is my blood" are intended more to change the people present than to change the bread and wine.

For him it was more important that the people became the real presence of God, that they became food and drink for the world, than that the bread and wine did.

That is, in fact, the real task of the Eucharist: to change people, to create out of us the real presence.

But this involves a painful breaking down of all that keeps us apart. At a Eucharist we may not protect ourselves. Our hurts and hates must be revealed and absorbed. When this happens hearts of stone will turn to hearts of flesh, bitterness to charity.

But livelier liturgies, better homilies and more singing will not, by themselves, bring that about. The complaint that liturgy is meaningless goes deeper. At its root lies the fact that people will celebrate as a community only when self-protectiveness, mutual suspicion and macho posturing are first broken down. But that requires new birth.

In birth, there are tears and anguish. Before the real dance comes the anguish.

8

RECEIVING THE SPIRIT FOR OUR OWN LIVES: THE PASCHAL MYSTERY, WAITING AND CHASTITY

If we die before we die we come to freedom . . . for the future belongs to those who have nothing left to lose.

(MARY-JO LEDDY)

Paschal Death: Letting Go

IT IS CRUEL to talk about death, but crueler still not to. Adult life is not child's life. As adults we are asked to die and, like Christ, we sweat blood about it. Physical death is only one part of it.

We are dying all the time, struggling painfully to let go of youth, health, daydreams and possible dreams, infatuations, romances, honeymoons and, in the end, of life itself. No one lets go easily.

Ernest Becker contends that the denial of death is the primary repression within Western culture and that from that repression come the majority of our psychological ailments. He is right.

We do not accept death. We deny, daydream, mummify, pretend, cling, drug, refuse to wake up, and do everything except accept that we must let go.

Two images describe us. The first is that of Mary Magdala on Easter morning wanting desperately to cling to the Jesus she had known rather than accepting the resurrected one. The second is that of mummification. Like the ancient Egyptians who reacted to death by embalming and mummifying their dead, we tend to embalm and mummify what has died in us.

The proper response to death in all its kinds is not these postures, but the acceptance of the paschal mystery. But this needs to be explained.

As Christians we need to distinguish between two kinds of death, *paschal* and *terminal*.

Terminal death is a death that ends life, ends possibilities. It brings dreams, health, honeymoons and happiness to final closure. *Paschal death* is real death. Something precious dies. However in this kind of death there is an opening to new life and new spirit.

In paschal death there is always a birth as well, just as in childbirth a woman also loses her child in giving it birth.

The paschal mystery, the passage through death to new life, though normally associated with Christ's death and resurrection, is in its widest sense a natural mystery. All reality grows and deepens through it.

Christ's life, however, offers its deepest modeling, and his death and resurrection are a paschal drama in which we can participate.

As an event in Christ's life, the paschal mystery has four distinct movements. Together these form one dynamic movement from death to life and together they form a psychology of love and growth.

In a very simple schema, the paschal mystery, as an event and as a psychology, might be charted as follows:

Passion and death	the loss of life
Resurrection	the reception of new life
Ascension	the refusal to cling, as ascending beyond the old life
Pentecost	the reception of new spirit for the new life

What does all this mean concretely? It can best be understood through a series of stories.

A priest I know tells the story of a family whose father

was dying of cancer. Big, tough, a welder, the man was not dying easily. For months he hung on, long after there was any hope. In intense pain, his body wasted away, the disease terminal, he still refused to die. He lay clinging to life. Each day his family spent their time with him.

One day the eldest son sat by the bedside watching his dad's suffering. Overcome by the pain and hopelessness of it, he squeezed his hand and said, "Dad, die for God's sake! Let go! It's got to be better there than here."

Almost immediately his dad became calm and within minutes he died. The words his son spoke were paschal words, Christian words, words that trust God enough to be able to die in him and know that new life and new spirit will be born in the dying.

When King David's illegitimate son was dying, David put on sackcloth and began to fast and pray, begging God to save his son. However messengers arrive and David learns that his son is already dead. Upon hearing this he immediately puts aside the sackcloth and prayer and goes to his house where he bathes, anoints himself, eats, drinks, then sleeps with his wife, who conceives a new life, Solomon.

When he senses that he has scandalized those around him who feel he has not properly mourned his son, David speaks paschal words: "While the child was alive I fasted and prayed, imploring God to save the child. Now the child is dead. I must move on to create new life."

When we stop clinging, when we give ourselves over to God in trust, new life will be conceived and new spirit will be released. Death will be paschal and not terminal.

Paschal Mystery: The New You

NOTHING IN OUR CULTURE prepares us to die. Invariably death takes us as conqueror, against our will. We protest, grow bitter, bargain for time, give in to anger, and are eventually dragged protesting out of life.

There is little within us which empowers us to let go peacefully, with some grace, and surrender life in gratitude for what has been and in hope for what will be.

This is true not just of physical death, but of all the types of death that impale themselves upon us. Invariably, they catch us unprepared.

I have already mentioned the refusal to cling as an entry into the paschal mystery, namely into the kind of death which is an opening to new life and to the reception of new spirit.

I want now to illustrate that it is the refusal to let go and to enter death in trust, the refusal to enter the paschal mystery, that is the cause of so much unhappiness, bitterness and despair in our lives.

The first example concerns the death of our youth, health and sexual attractiveness. For many of us, long before we have to surrender our lives in death, we are forced to surrender these in a different kind of death.

Youth, health and sexual attractiveness are gifts from God, but they do not last. Their loss is a real death, especially in a culture such as our own in which you have a place in the mainstream only if you possess them. For this reason, we do not let them go easily. We cling.

Like the ancient Egyptians, we attempt to mummify our youth and sexual attractiveness through contemporary forms of "embalming": cosmetics, dyes, face lifts, pretense and lies about our age.

When we are fifty, sixty, seventy—or forty—and trying to be twenty, someone must challenge us: "Let go, for God's sake! Be your age, it will be better then than it is now!"

Old age is hell for those who cling and want to be young at all costs. It can be peaceful and full of joys, if we are willing to receive its spirit.

God always gives us new life. We never die.

Whenever something passes, be it youth, health or sexual attractiveness, something else takes its place. With that something else, God also sends a new spirit, a new Pentecost.

However if, like Mary Magdala, we are unwilling to let go of what is gone, then there can be no ascension to new life and no new Pentecost of new spirit.

Entry into the paschal mystery, namely into the death that brings new life, new love, new friendship, new health, new attractiveness, new meaning and new depth, requires that we die, that we accept new life, and that we refuse to cling so that new life can ascend and new spirit can be given us.

Ultimately this depends upon trust. We must trust God enough to let ourselves die, to stop clinging, to believe that God will always give us something new and something better.

We must trust God enough to believe that nothing worthwhile will ever be lost and that he makes all things new. This also holds true for our lives of love and friendship. When we first meet, when love is young, there is a period of infatua-

tion, of emotional electricity, of honeymoon. But all relationships grow and change and all honeymoons end.

Too often when the honeymoon ends the love begins to
die, to grow sour, bland and resentful. Almost always a large
part of the problem is the unwillingness to enter the paschal
mystery. After the honeymoon, loves and friendships, like Jesus,
need to rise on the third day, ascend to a new level, and release a new and deeper spirit.

This is also true for our dreams and hopes. When we go
through life refusing to let go of a hope that can never be for
us, when we refuse to accept that we are not as physically attractive, slim, athletic, talented, bright, unblemished, strong
and connected as we would like to be, then we will always
live in resentment and bitterness, frustrated and caught up in
a daydream which prevents us from living by constantly saying "if only . . ."

In that daydream we can never be happy because we are
refusing to accept the spirit that God has given us for our
own life.

By refusing to die paschally to false dreams, we never in
gratitude and joy pick up our own lives.

How happy the person who accepts his or her life as it is
with the spirit God has given for it!

Pentecost—a Need for Our Lives

WE GO THROUGH LIFE struggling. This is true for everyone. We all live with inferiorities, dashed dreams and deep frustrations. Because of this we tend to grow jealous. We begin to envy other people's lives, seeing in their lives the things that we are missing within our own.

This increases our disappointment with who we are and, all too often, puts us into an attitude within which we refuse to accept what is good, happy, creative, and pleasurable within our own lives.

Instead of picking up our own lives and living them creatively, we put them on hold. We focus on something we are missing, and desperately crave—a marriage partner, a certain friendship, a certain achievement, a certain prestige, a certain physical appearance, a certain fame or place to live—and we relativize and belittle our own lives to the point of finding them unhappy and meaningless.

We live in brackets, waiting; always waiting for this certain something to come along and fulfill our lives. When this happens, a deep restlessness sets in. There is a beautiful image in Scripture that depicts this. After the resurrection of Jesus his disciples are unable to pick up the spirit of his new presence. They want instead to have their old, earthly Jesus back. Eventually they are reduced to huddling in fear in a locked room, paralyzed. When they receive the Spirit of the resurrected Christ they burst from that room, now alive with the Spirit for their actual lives.

When we live in restless unhappiness, not satisfied with our situation in life because we are unmarried, or because we are not married to whom we would like to be, or because we would have liked a different job or different family or different body, a different set of friends or a different city to live in, we live, like the apostles, huddled in fear.

Let me illustrate this with an example from Brian Moore's novel *The Lonely Passion of Judith Hearne*.

Judith, a woman approaching menopause, is bright, talented, educated, artistic and gifted with a pleasant personality and pleasant looks. But she desperately wants to be married. She is deeply frustrated with being single and does not consider herself a complete person. Consciously and unconsciously, her whole life is geared toward finding a husband.

Because of this, her entire present life has little meaning or satisfaction for her. She wants to be married and has decided that, for her, there can be no meaning, no genuine reality, outside that.

Early in the story she meets a man who interests her, and who she senses is interested in her. He is a pleasant man, though also a calculating schemer and dilettante. It is soon apparent to the reader that Judith would be taken for a ride in this marriage. However, because she is desperate and this is a real chance at marriage, Judith pursues the relationship and, in a vague kind of way, falls in love.

On his part, the man sees her as a possible business partner, as someone whose money he could use.

At a certain point Judith proposes to him. She is rejected and the disappointment, coupled with the hurt of rejection, triggers within her a deep depression which takes her on an alcoholic binge and eventually leads to a nervous breakdown and a mental hospital. The story climaxes with her ex-boyfriend coming to visit her in the hospital and announcing that he has changed his mind and wants to marry her after all. She refuses and in her explanation to him we learn things to help us understand the connection between Ascension and Pentecost. These are her words:

When you are a little girl you dream of the perfect man, of that perfect person who will make you whole, who will give you reality. He will be handsome, and good, and kind and generous. He will be perfect. Then, as you get older, you revise your expectations downward. After a while, he doesn't have to be so perfect, or handsome, or good. Finally, when you get to be my age, he doesn't have to be handsome, good, or loving at all. Anyone will do—even if they are common as dirt! You'll take anyone because you think that, alone, you aren't anything.

But I've learned something here. I've grown to know that, even alone, single, just by myself, I am something! I have reality!

She throws his address card away as she leaves the hospital and we see in her face that she is now a woman of inner strength and inner joy. She has a new calmness, attractiveness and energy. The restlessness is gone. She has received the spirit of her own life. You sense too that, if she wants to, she will easily find someone good to marry, now that she no longer desperately needs to.

Pentecost is not an abstract mystery. We are asked to accept the spirit of our actual lives. When we do this, then we no longer belittle our own lives but, like Judith Hearne, know that even with all our inferiorities and frustrations, just by ourselves, we are something.

Mary Magdala's Easter Prayer

I never suspected
   Resurrection
     and to be so painful
     to leave me weeping
With joy
   to have met you, alive and smiling, outside an empty
     tomb
With regret
   not because I've lost you
   but because I've lost you in how I had you—
     in understandable, touchable, kissable, clingable
       flesh
     not as fully Lord, but as graspably human.

I want to cling, despite your protest
   cling to your body
   cling to your, and my, clingable humanity
   cling to what we had, our past.

But I know that . . . if I cling
   you cannot ascend and
   I will be left clinging to your former self
   . . . unable to receive your present spirit.

The Value of Fasting and Feasting

WE CELEBRATE FEASTS differently than we used to. Formerly there was generally a long fast leading up to a feast, and a joyous celebration afterward. Today, usually, there is a long celebration leading up to the feast, and a fast afterward.

The way we celebrate Christmas exemplifies this. Nearly two months before the actual day, we begin to celebrate. The parties start, the decorations and lights go up, the cards go out, and the Christmas music begins to play.

When Christmas Day finally arrives we are already satiated with the specialness of the season, tired, over-saturated with celebration and ready to move on. By then we are ready to go back to ordinary life, and even to do some fasting . . . having had enough of turkey dinners! The Christmas season used to last until February. Now, realistically, it is over on December 25th.

This is a curious reversal. Traditionally the build-up was always toward a feast, celebration came after. Today the feast is first, the fast comes after.

Why is this? And, are we the better or the worse for reversing the fast-feast cycle?

A colleague of mine commented that our society knows how to anticipate an event, but not how to sustain it. That is only partially true. The real issue is not so much that we do not know how to sustain something, we do not know precisely how to anticipate something. We confuse anticipation with celebration itself.

One of our weaknesses today is that we find it hard to live in the face of any anticipation, inconsummation or un-fulfilled tension without moving swiftly to resolve it. Longing and fasting are not our strong points. Because we cannot build properly toward a feast, we cannot celebrate properly either.

Celebration is an organic process. To feast, one must first fast; to come to consummation, one must first live in chastity; and to taste specialness one must first have a sense of what is ordinary. When fasting, inconsummation and the dour rhythm of the ordinary are short-circuited, then fatigue of the spirit, boredom, and disappointment replace celebration. We are left with the empty feeling which says "All this hype, for this!" Something can only be sublime if, first of all, there is some sublimation.

I am old enough to have known another time. Like our own, this time too had its faults, but it also had its strengths. One of these strengths was its belief, a lived belief, that feasting depends upon prior fasting, that the sublime depends upon a prerequisite sublimation.

I have vivid memories of the Advents and Lents of my childhood. How strict those times were! They were seasons of fast and renunciation: no weddings, no dances, fewer parties, fewer drinks, fewer desserts, and generally less of everything that constitutes specialness and celebration. Churches were draped in purple and statues covered. The colors were dark and the mood penitential; but the feasts that followed, Easter and Christmas, were oh, so special!

Perhaps I am wafting nostalgia; after all, I was young then, naïve and deprived, and thus able to meet Christmas and Easter, and other celebrations, with a fresher spirit. That may be, but the specialness that surrounded feasts has died for another, more important reason, namely we do not anticipate them properly any more.

We short-circuit fasting, inconsummation and the prerequisite longing. Simply put, how can Christmas be special when we arrive at December 25th exhausted from weeks of Christmas parties? How can Easter be special when we treat Lent just as we treat any other season? How indeed can anything be sublime when we have all but lost our capacity for sublimation?

Celebration, as mentioned earlier, is an organic process. It is created by a dynamic interplay between anticipation and fulfillment, longing and inconsummation, ordinary and special, work and play.

Life, love and sexuality must be celebrated within that fast-feast rhythm. Seasons of play must follow seasons of work, seasons of consummation are contingent upon seasons of longing, and seasons of intimacy can only grow out of seasons of solitude.

Presence depends upon absence, intimacy upon solitude, play upon work. Even God rested only after working for six days!

Today the absence of genuine specialness and enjoyment within our lives is due largely to the breakdown of this rhythm. In a word, Christmas is no longer special because we have celebrated it during Advent, weddings are no longer special because we have already slept with the bride, and experiences of all kinds are often flat, boring and unable to excite us because we had them prematurely.

Premature experience is bad precisely because it is premature. To celebrate Christmas during Advent, to celebrate

Easter without fasting, to short-circuit longing in any area, is, like sleeping with the bride before the wedding, a fault in chastity. All premature experience has the effect of draining us of great enthusiasm and great expectations (which can only be built up through sublimation, tension and painful waiting).

Virgin Birth

The perennial paradox
Peculiar to this Father and Son
Specialists in confounding
Human wisdom withdrawn from wonder.
A virgin gives birth
Not to sterility but
To a Messiah.

Now what has virginity to do with giving birth?
Nothing!
When wisdom wastes words wandering
    towards the truth that will not set you free.

Virginity and inconsummation
    incomplete heart and flesh
    wrestling with a God who has no flesh
    and who won't let flesh
    meet flesh
Aches, waiting completeness
To stave off sterility
Truly the unforgivable sin against
The spirit of life which is holy.

But sterility becomes pregnant
    with yearning
    for the spirit that sleeps

with God in the night
and impregnates with messianic spirit
those patient enough to yearn
and sweat lonely tears
rather than ruin gift
with impatience.

Only virgins' wombs bring forth messiahs
They alone live in advent
   waiting, a delaying bridegroom
   late, hopelessly, beyond the 11th hour.
Still, the virgin's womb waits
Refusing all counterfeit lovers and
   all impatience
   which demands
   flesh on flesh and
   a divine kingdom on human terms.

Messiahs are only born
   in virginity's space
   within virginity's patience
   which lets
   God be God
   and
   love be gift.

RONALD ROLHEISER, OMI
DECEMBER 14TH, 1981

9

IN WEAKNESS, STRENGTH

It is not always easy for us to distinguish
between a moment of dying and a moment
of new birth.

(ALAN JONES)

Weakness Leads to Strength

A FEW YEARS AGO I was given a very mixed blessing: I got sick. Oh, I had been sick before: the usual acceptable sort of things, appendicitis, a couple of ripped-up knees from sports, colds and viruses. This time it was different. The physical cause was not so evident. I had ulcers! I lost some weight, some friends and a lot of self-confidence. Ulcers, or so it is believed, are caused by psychosomatic factors. Translated, that means that super-normal folks should not have them. You get them and your friends start wondering about you and you start wondering about yourself. You examine your lifestyle, your work, your emotions, your relationships.

You look at a whole lot of things differently and sense that others are looking at you differently: Is he really sick? Is he a hypochondriac? Does he want to be sick? He was always so intense I knew that this would happen! He is unhappy in his state in life! He is simply looking for attention and sympathy! There is something he cannot face!

You pick up the reactions and soon you begin to ask yourself the same things. It all gets frightening because you do not know the answers and, deep down, you sense that any or all of those things could be true.

We are pretty complex critters! The physical illness is not all that serious, but you get pretty serious. Well, not at first. First you do the normal things. You see doctors, hopeful always that some medicine or treatment will very quickly restore you to normal health. Then as time drags, and you do not get better, and friends no longer seem concerned (or are perhaps even suspicious), you get angry and impatient: with doctors, with medicines, with friends, with yourself.

Then, when that does not help, your strength begins to break and for the first time you are actually sick. Initially the symptoms are all bad: self-pity, anger at friends, impatience with everything. Your old confidence and strength is gone. At this stage you are genuinely ill, though the physical illness has been mostly lost in the new emotional lesions.

But things slowly change. Ulcers heal, the scars disappear; first the physical ones, and later, much more slowly, the emotional ones. You feel strength again and old friends and old circles begin to open up again.

Health returns but it is different. Some of the old self-confidence is gone, replaced by a new sense of vulnerability and relativity that is immensely freeing.

You realize more clearly what is gift and what is earned. You know that you, on your own, cannot guarantee your own health, nor your attractiveness and desirability in love and friendship.

Stripped naked, weakened, and greatly humbled, you stop fighting, first because you are defeated, but later, when strength and resources return, because you realize that there is no reason to fight.

Life, health, love, it is all pure gift! You take less for granted and your old need to perform, to achieve, to dominate, to possess and impress, to win by effort what can only be received as gift, has been dealt a blow. It is painful, but freeing: painful because you realize that there is so little you can do; freeing because you realize that there is so little you have to do.

You begin to beg for conversion (even as you sense how difficult it is) because you would want to transvaluate all your values and priorities, your whole self, and begin life anew.

Even so, you know you are still a long way from home. There is still a lot of turf between you and the promised land. But, like Moses and Abraham, you have been given a "glimpse from afar."

When one is wandering in a wilderness it is helpful to know in what direction the milk and honey lies. You will still spend most of your life wandering, wondering how to enter the promised land. But with an anonymous poet from the past, you realize that God is finally taking you in hand:

> I asked for strength that I might achieve;
> I was made weak, that I might learn humbly to obey.
>
> I asked for health, that I might do greater things;
> I was given infirmity, that I might do better things.
>
> I asked for riches, that I might be happy;
> I was given poverty, that I might be free . . .
>
> I asked for power, that I might have praise from men;
> I was given weakness, that I might feel the need for
>   God.
>
> I asked for all things that I might enjoy life;
> I was given life, that I might enjoy all things.
>
> I got nothing I asked for, but everything that I had
>   hoped for.
> Almost despite myself, my unspoken prayers were
>   answered.
> I am among all men the most richly blessed.

Keep passing the open windows!

Jesus Was a Good Loser

IT IS HARD FOR US to love each other. Our relationships are too charged with competition, jealousy and violence.

Win! Be the best at something! Show others you are more talented and classier than they are! Leave the competition behind! Strut your stuff! Winning is not everything, it is the only thing! Show me a good loser and I will show you a loser.

These phrases are not merely cheerleaders' rhetoric meant to inspire us to do better things, they are viruses infecting our culture and psyches. From infancy we are infected with the drive to out-do, to out-achieve and to out-hustle each other. From this comes competition, violence and jealousy.

We structure our lives around competition and most of our meaning comes from achieving. When we achieve, win, are better than others at something, our lives seem fuller. Our self-image inflates and we feel confident and worthwhile. Conversely when we cannot stand out, when we are just another face in the crowd, we struggle to maintain a healthy self-image.

In either case we struggle continually with jealousy and dissatisfaction. We envy and secretly hate the talented, the beautiful, the powerful, the rich, the achievers, the famous, the winners. Moreover we make ourselves miserable by constantly comparing our own lack of talent, beauty and achievement with their successes.

We were infected with this disease, unhealthy competitiveness, when we were still very young. From the time we started school, and even before, everything around us (and many things within us) pushed us to achieve, to set ourselves apart from others. So we pushed ourselves to stand out, to be at the top of the class, to be the best athlete, the best dressed, the best-looking, the most musically talented, the most popular, the most experienced, the most traveled, the one who knew the most about cars or movies or history or sex or the stars, or whatever.

At all costs the drive was to find something at which we could beat others. At all costs the idea was somehow to set ourselves apart and above.

That idea is deeply rooted in us. Because of it, our relationships are too charged with violence, competition and jealousy. How can we love each other and accept each person in respect and equality when we must first out-achieve each other?

How can we love each other when every achievement is cause for jealousy and resentment? How can we love each other when an overly competitive spirit makes us unable to see with the heart and the mind of Christ?

To love is to be vulnerable. To love is to see the other as equal. To love is to let others' talents and achievements enhance our lives. But we are generally incapable of these things.

We are too infected with competition to allow ourselves to be vulnerable, to see others as equals and not to let the achievements and talents of others threaten us. Because of this we develop our talents, not to share our gifts and enhance others' lives, but to measure ourselves, to strut our wares, to stand out. Likewise, because of this, we divide people into two groups, winners and losers, achievers and failures. We admire and hate the former and despise the latter.

Because of this also we are constantly sizing up each other, rating bodies, hair, intelligence, clothing, talents and achievements. As we rate, we become unhealthily depressed when others outscore us and unhealthily inflated when we appear superior to them.

The enigma separating us from each other becomes ever more difficult to penetrate as we become more and more obsessed with ourselves and our need to be special, to sit above. We live in jealousy, competition and violence. The other is perennially perceived as a threat.

We need to let the mind and heart of Christ exorcise this demon from our lives.

In the mind and heart of Christ we will perceive ways of relating beyond competition, jealousy and violence. In the mind and heart of Christ there is no need to stand out and be special. There the other's special talents are not seen as a threat but as something which enhances all of life, our life included.

What is the mind and heart of Christ? It is the acceptance of the fact that everyone is special and therefore all are equal. Nobody sits above the rest and nobody has a right to feel that he or she should sit above the rest. This is true for nations as well as for individuals.

If individuals accepted this there would be much less jealousy, competition and violence among us. If nations accepted it, our world would not be poised on the brink of economic and nuclear destruction.

Show me a good loser and I will show you a loser! Jesus was a good loser. In his under-achieving we all achieved salvation. In his mind and heart lie the seeds that can bind us into one heart beyond jealousy, competition and violence.

The Dignity of Honesty

ONE OF THE most debilitating aspects of life today is that we do not admit to each other the cost of struggle. Our real fears are seldom allowed to surface.

Yet we all struggle.

Our lives are full of pain, little comes easy for us, and we make a living, remain healthy, remain attractive and achieve success only at great cost. Fear is always present. The fear of failure, of slipping, of letting others see that life and success are not automatic, that life is lived at the edges of sickness, unattractiveness, boredom, failure and sadness.

However, we bury and hide struggle and fear. Rarely do we genuinely share how we really feel, what our fears are, and how difficult it is to be who we are. Rarely do we admit anyone into our inner space where fear, struggle and inadequacy make themselves felt.

We all go through life posturing strength, pretending; lying really, giving the impression that all is easy and that friendship, health, achievement and attractiveness are easeful and automatic.

But that is dishonest and debilitating. Dishonest because it is not true. God knows, and we know, how precariously we are glued together!

It is debilitating because when we are forced to hide our pain and fear, we are forced too to hide the very strands within which compassion can be found. In shared weakness and fear there is a common meeting ground.

Our weakness and fears, much more than our achievements and successes, drive us inward and put us in touch with what is deepest, softest and most worthwhile within the heart. In that part of the heart we discover who we really are and there we understand that we are not what we achieve, but what is given to us.

Outside that, when we posture strength and lie and pretend, we learn falsely that life is not a gift to be shared, but a possession to be defended.

The road to love and intimacy lies in a compassion born out of the perception of shared struggle and shared fear. When we genuinely see another's wound and struggle, then that other enters a deeper, more real, part of us.

But it is precisely here that the problem lies. More than anything else, we struggle not to reveal our pain and fears to others, for we have been falsely taught that community and love are grounded upon something else, namely upon impressing each other. Perhaps the greatest obstacle to intimacy and community is that propensity to believe that others will love us only when we are impressive and strong.

Because of this, we go through life trying to impress others into liking us. Rather than sharing ourselves as we really are—vulnerable, tender, struggling, full of fear—we try to be so sensational that there can be no possible reason not to love us.

Like the inhabitants of Babel, we try to build a tower that is so impressive that we overpower others. The result for us, as the result then, is counterproductive. Because of pretense, we go through life "speaking different languages," that is, unable to find a common meeting ground upon which to understand each other. Understanding takes place through compassion and compassion is itself the fruit of shared vulnerability.

Thus, as long as we hide our struggles and fears, we will not find intimacy. When fears and struggle are hidden, when achievement, health, attractiveness and friendship are projected as automatic, then our talents, intelligence, wit, charms, beauty, and artistic and athletic abilities cannot be seen for what they are intended to be, namely beautiful gifts which enrich life.

They are projected, then, as objects of envy and they become forces which create jealousy and further wound.

When there is no shared vulnerability life becomes what we can achieve, and our talents are possessions to be defended. We must therefore admit to each other the cost of struggle. Our real fears must be allowed to surface. Intimacy lies in that.

Intimacy will be achieved only when we are so vulnerable that others can see that we share with them a common condition.

Scripture reminds us that here, in this life, we see each other as less than fully real—"as through a glass, darkly, an enigma."

We contribute to the enigma, we make ourselves less real, precisely to the extent that we do not admit to each other that it is hard for us. It is only when we see each other's fears and struggles that we become real to each other. The path home, out of exile, lies in vulnerability.

The threads of compassion and a concomitant intimacy will appear automatically when we present ourselves as we really are, without false props, as tender.

People Do Not Break Easily

DAN BERRIGAN commented that if Jesus returned to earth he would take a whip and drive out both patients and doctors from all counseling and psychologists' offices with the words: "Take up your couch and walk! You've been given skin to survive in this world!"

There is wisdom and challenge in those words.

God covered our nerves with skin, we are not so hypersensitive. He has also given us a remarkable resiliency and an incredible capacity to heal. We are tougher and more elastic than we actually think.

I remember my first surprising reminder of this. As a young child playing hockey I was bullied and hit by a bigger kid. I fell and began to cry, convinced that I was seriously hurt. I waited vainly for the world to stop and for everyone to come and examine my hurt. But the game went on and I lay on the ice, ignored, until someone came and challenged me with the fact that I was not really hurt, I was only feeling sorry for myself and was quite capable, if I wanted to, of continuing to play. It came as a surprise to realize that I was not so fragile after all. I could take a lick. It was humiliating, to be sure, but I was quite capable of bouncing back.

As we get older the games, the bullying and the hurts become less physical, more psychological, more sophisticated. But one dynamic remains constant, most often we are not as hurt as we think. Invariably there is more self-pity than actual wound.

As human beings we are in fact gifted with an incredible

resiliency. Skin, bones, psyches, hearts, when pushed to it, have a remarkable bounce. They do not break easily, and when they do they have an unbelievable capacity to heal.

We can take a fall, a hurt, a cut, a rejection. It does not kill us, we heal, there is seldom an excuse for paralysis, never one for despair. We are tougher than we think.

It is when we forget this that we get ourselves into trouble and find ourselves far away from the feast, happiness and celebration that God has put at the heart of life.

The most incredible and challenging of all Christ's teachings is that we can in fact be happy, that we can celebrate and enjoy life, even though we and the world we live in are far from perfect. Mostly we do not believe this.

Mostly we go through life protesting our right to despair, partly paralyzed by self-pity and limping when there is not enough reason to limp. Silently or out loud, we tell God and others: "If you knew how much I have been hurt, you wouldn't tell me that I can be happy! If you only knew how fragile I am! If you only knew how sensitive I am and how easily I can be hurt! If you only knew how unfair it is for me. If you only knew how I have been rejected! If you only knew . . . ! It is too late for me. I am too wounded!"

But that posture and attitude is, in the end, a form of self-pity, a mini-masturbation which sells us short. It sells God short too for he endowed us with more than that. He gave us more resiliency, more bounce, more toughness, more capacity for healing and, God knows, more reason to hope than we allow ourselves in our hypersensitivity.

It is good to be sensitive, but too often we are hypersensitive. We think our bones are broken when they are not, that our psyches and hearts have no bounce when they do, that a wound will never heal when it will, and that we are paralyzed when we are not.

So we limp or lie down and offer a myriad of excuses which explain why we cannot be happy.

The challenge is needed: take up your couch and walk, you have been given skin! We are tougher than we give ourselves credit for.

Knowing this should help us move out toward celebration, beyond our hurts. With the elasticity of body, psyche and heart that God has given us we are not allowed to despair. Ultimately we can absorb anything and bounce back.

Because of this we are allowed to make some mistakes and to take some bad falls. We will get hurt, but we may never say "I hurt too much to enter the game of celebration again. I am beyond healing!" We are never beyond healing.

Christ's challenge to celebrate is uncompromising. It challenges us to our own capacities, to our own toughness, to love beyond hurt. It challenges us to risk great hurt.

Nikos Kazantzakis starts his autobiography with these words: "Three kinds of souls, three prayers: 1) I am a bow in your hands, Lord, draw me, lest I rot. 2) Do not overdraw me, Lord, I shall break. 3) Overdraw me, Lord, and who cares if I break!"

When we know how resilient God has made us, we risk the third prayer.

Life Is a Messy Business

ATHEISTIC PHILOSOPHER Maurice Merleau-Ponty did not believe in God. The reason, he stated, is because ambiguity is the fundamental phenomenological fact within our existence and a belief in God is not consistent with that experience.

That phrase, in an abstract way, expresses something we all experience, namely life is utterly messy; so messy in fact that it can leave one wondering whether indeed there exists an all-powerful and caring God. Nobody goes through life antiseptically without dirt, pain, mess and death.

But, unlike Merleau-Ponty, I believe in God precisely for that reason. Life may be messy but it is real, not plastic. We are not Swiss clocks, infallibly ordered, made to tick meticulously, precise and antiseptic. Rather our lives are anything but ordered and clocklike. We cannot live without messiness, complications and much emotional and physical pain.

It begins when we are born. Birth is a messy process which causes pain, dictates involvement and complicates peoples' lives irrevocably. Living does too!

Work, interrelations, love, sex, friendship, aging, all of these are complex, earthy, messy businesses which are always at least partially full of pain, pettiness, limit, compromise and death. They are full of joy and meaning too, but these are seldom given purely. Moreover no one goes through life without having his or her dignity, freedom and dreams frustrated and stepped on. There is no antiseptic route through life.

The whiteness of our baptismal robes, the purity of our hearts, minds, and bodies, and the freshness of our youth, sully and dirty and bear the stain of living.

As we grow older Gerard Manley Hopkins' words ring ever more true:

> And all is smeared with trade; bleared, smeared with
> toil;
> And wears man's smudge and shares man's smell: the
> soil . . .

Often this leaves us discouraged and questioning. More seriously, this often leads to a subtle despair. Stated simply the algebra of this despair, and ultimately of all despair, reads like this: If all is muddled, then all is permitted.

That attitude is viral and deadly. It is perhaps the worst temptation faced by an adult. Because of it we sell ourselves out, give up, throw dignity and dreams to the wind and settle for second best. This single factor is perhaps at the root of most of the infidelity, sexual irresponsibility, and unbelief within our culture.

When we sell out our dignity and dreams, then, like Merleau-Ponty, we will have trouble experiencing God. The Highest is more clearly experienced when we are giving ourselves over to what is highest.

The messiness of life also leaves us tempted in another way, namely to try to live antiseptically.

Since we cannot live and love deeply without hurting, without pettiness, enslaving and humiliating entanglements, without smear, we opt not to live and love deeply at all. So we hang loose, refusing depth. We stay away from all that might hurt—or heal—us deeply.

In doing this we make life plastic—antiseptic, clean, without dirt and smell but totally lifeless and without meaning, like a plastic rose. We need to accept the contours of our existence.

We are not angels, free, soaring spirits, unencumbered by the limits of time and flesh. Our souls are born enfleshed in soil, pain, blood and smell. We were never intended to be angels.

But with that comes a special dignity, the dignity that a real rose possesses over a plastic one.

Peter Meinke wrote a sonnet honoring the death of the man who invented the plastic rose:

> The Man who invented the plastic rose is dead,
> behold his mark.
> His undying flawless blossoms never close
> But guard his grave unbending through the dark.
> He understood neither beauty nor flowers,
> Which catch our hearts in nets as soft as sky
> And bind us with a thread of fragile hours;
> Flowers are beautiful because they die.
> Beauty without the perishable pulse
> is dry and sterile, an abandoned stage
> With false forests. But the results
> Support this man's invention: He knew his age;
> A vision of our tearless time discloses
> Artificial men sniffing plastic roses.
>
> *Ladies' Home Journal*, 1964

10

&

THE BOSOM OF GOD IS NOT A GHETTO: CATHOLICITY AND JUSTICE

When we come to the end of our pilgrimage and reach heaven, God will ask, "Where are the others?"

(CHARLES PEGUY)

A Heart with One Room

OUR AGE is witnessing an erosion of Catholicism. The consequence of this, besides our drab somberness, is a polarization which, both in the world and in the church, is rendering us incapable of working together against the problems which threaten us all. Let me explain.

We are, I submit, becoming ever less Catholic. What is implied here? What is slipping? What does it mean to be Catholic?

The opposite of Catholic is not Protestant. All Christians, Protestants or Roman Catholics, characterize their faith as Catholic—as well as one, holy and apostolic.

The word Catholic means universal, wide. It speaks of a comprehensive embrace. Its opposite, therefore, is narrowness, pettiness, lack of openness, sectarianism, provincialism, factionalism, fundamentalism and ideology.

To my mind, the best definition of the word Catholic comes from Jesus himself, who tells us: "In my Father's house there are many rooms" (John 14:2).

In speaking of the Father's house, Jesus is not pointing to a mansion in the sky, but to God's heart. God's heart has many rooms. It can embrace everything. It is wide, unpetty, open and antithetical to all that is factional, fundamentalistic and ideological. It is a heart that does not divide things up according to ours and theirs.

Nikos Kazantzakis wrote: "The bosom of God is not a

ghetto." That is another way of saying that God has a Catholic heart.

To affirm this, however, is not to say that, since God is open to all and embraces all, nothing makes any difference; we may do as we like, all morality is relative, all beliefs are equal, and nobody may lay claim to truth.

There is a false concept of openness which affirms that to embrace all means to render all equal. Jesus belies this. He affirms the universal embrace of God's heart without affirming, as a consequence, that everything is OK. His Father loves everyone, even as he discriminates between right and wrong.

Catholicism can be spoken of as slipping, in that, unlike God's heart, more and more it seems, our hearts have just one room.

Today we are seeing a creeping narrowness and intolerance. Fundamentalism, with its many types of ideology, has infected us. This is as true in the secular world as in the church. Fundamentalism and the narrowness and consequent polarization it spawns are everywhere. But this needs to be understood.

We tend to think of fundamentalism as a conservative view which takes Scripture so literally as to be unable to relate to the world in a realistic way. But that is just one, and a very small, kind of fundamentalism. We see fundamentalism wherever we see a heart with just one room.

The characteristic of all fundamentalism is that, precisely, it seizes onto some fundamental value, for example the wisdom of the past, the divine inspiration of Scripture or the importance of justice and equality, and makes that the sole criterion for judging goodness and authenticity.

In that sense, the fundamentalist's heart has just one room—a conservative, liberal, biblical, charismatic, feminist, anti-feminist, social justice, anti-abortion or pro-choice room. It judges you as good, acceptable, decent, sincere, Christian, loving and worth listening to only if you are in that room. If you are not ideologically committed to that fundamental, complete with all the prescribed rhetoric and accepted indignations, then you are judged as insincere or ignorant, and in need of either conversion or of having your consciousness raised.

In the end, all fundamentalism is ideology and all ideology is fundamentalism—and both are a heart with one room, a bosom that is a ghetto.

That is the real un-Catholicism.

Tragically too, at the heart of all fundamentalism and ideology, there is an absence of a healthy self-love and a healthy self-criticism. That is why fundamentalists and ideologues are all so defensive, hypersensitive and humorless.

It is because of this that the world and the church are so full of intolerance, anger, lack of openness, self-righteous condemnation, scapegoating and academic and moral intimidation. There are too few rooms in our hearts!

Given this, it is not surprising that very little genuine dialogue ever takes place. Most attempts at it are little more than name-calling and cheerleading. Given this too, it is not surprising that the working out of personal neuroses is frequently confused with genuine commitment to causes.

In God's house there are many rooms. There is an embrace for everyone; rich and poor, conservative and liberal, irrespective of whether one is wearing silks or denims. God's house is a Catholic house.

And "we must be Catholic as our heavenly Father is Catholic." We must create more Catholic hearts and more Catholic houses. And this is not a call to be wishy-washy relativists who affirm that everything is OK as long as you do it sincerely. Like Christ, we must discriminate between right and wrong and believe in a divine truth which judges the world.

But we must free ourselves from un-Catholicism, from fundamentalism and ideology which create a heart with just one room.

Closed to Love, Open to Hate

WE LIVE IN A TIME of pain and division. Daily, in the world and in the church, hatred, anger and bitterness are growing. It is ever harder to live at peace with each other, to be calm, not to alienate someone just by being. There is so much wound and division around. Women's issues, poverty and social justice, abortion, sexual morality, questions of leadership and authority, issues of war and peace, and styles of living and ministry are touching deep wounds and setting people bitterly against each other.

This is not even to mention issues such as personality conflicts, jealousy, greed and sin—which habitually divide.

Our psychic temperature is on the rise and with it, as Jesus predicted, son is turning against father, daughter against mother, sister against brother. We are being divided.

It is no longer possible to escape taking a stand on these issues, and to take a stand on them is to make enemies, to have someone hate you, to be accused of being narrow and to be alienated from other sincere persons. For anyone who is sensitive, this is the deepest pain of all.

Moreover none of us ever approaches these issues in complete fairness and objectivity. We are wounded, whether we admit it or not. Knowingly and unknowingly, in all these issues we have been either oppressor or oppressed and consequently we approach them either too full of wound or too defensive to see straight. In either case the temptation is to become bitter and to give in to the propensity to feel that we have the right to be angry, to hate certain people, to be self-righteous, and to dissociate sympathy and understanding from certain others.

That is a tragic mistake.

Valid, painful and imperative as these issues may be, reason, love, understanding and long-suffering may never give way to a progressive and militant bitterness which can irrevocably alienate. That is the road to hell because bitterness is hell.

Yet that is what is happening today. We are too easily giving in to the temptation to think that because we have been wounded, or because others are wounded, we have the right to hate, to withdraw our empathy, to think in terms of black and white, and to be bitter.

It is getting worse. Bitterness, like cancer, is slowly infecting more and more of Christ's body.

We need to read this, the sign of the times, and respond to it out of the Gospel. It is my submission that, given this bitterness, the Christian vocation today, for a time, will be that of letting ourselves bleed, in tears and tension, to wash out these wounds.

Let me illustrate what this means by way of an example. Just to be alive in the church today is to be caught in a painful tension. For example, the issues of women's rights and social justice are, without doubt, two of the primary challenges that the Holy Spirit is giving our age. Yet Rome refuses to raise seriously the question of the ordination of women and it silences Leonardo Boff, a voice for the poor. With that comes a wave of resentment, bitterness and hatred.

Daily I move in circles where people are bitter about these issues and I find myself increasingly reluctant to defend Rome's stance on them. On these two issues we are sitting on a powder keg and a deadly bitterness is flowing from them.

Yet no serious Catholic can be cavalier about the church as institution, as universal. Some 800 million Catholics cannot travel together without compromise, frustration, impatience, tears, rules and traditions which at times might seemingly strangle some of the life that the Holy Spirit is spawning.

When a universal church moves forward, it can only be in baby steps.

So what does the Christian who wants to be faithful today do? Ignore Rome? Consider the women's movement and social justice as fads? Grow cynical? Mind his or her own business and let be what is? Say "the hell with them all"?

Since nothing else is possible for now, save bitterness, which must be rejected, the answer lies in a fidelity which accepts suffering. To be faithful today means to live in pain, in tension, in frustration, in seeming compromise, often hated by both sides.

Our call today is to reconcile by feeling the pain of all sides and by letting our pain and helplessness be a buffer that heals, the blood that helps wash the wound. As a simple start we can test how open-minded we are on all these issues by seeing how much pain we are in. Not to be in pain is not to be open-minded.

It is a time of pain for the church, a time when we will all feel some hatred, a time when above all we must keep our peace of mind, our inner calm of spirit and our outer charity.

Most of all, it is time to resist bitterness and that hardness of spirit which dampens the Holy Spirit.

Social Justice and Contemplation

SOME YEARS AGO Ernst Kasemann, the Scripture scholar, commented that the problem with the church is that, chronically, the liberals aren't pious and the pious aren't liberal. If only, he speculated, Christians could be both.

Today, I submit, this dichotomy exists in the church between social justice and contemplation. Invariably those most actively involved in social justice are not as deeply involved in contemplation. Conversely those on the front lines of contemplation are often glaringly absent in the arena of social justice.

This situation, while far from ideal, would be more acceptable, given different charisms and calls, a division of labor, and the fact that nobody can be on the front lines of everything, except for the fact that, most often, there is suspicion and distrust between those who identify closely with one or the other of these.

Far from seeing each other as sister and brother in a common struggle, as persons with different charisms called to unblock different arteries within the body of Christ, more often than not these two spend more time fighting with each other than challenging a world which tends to ignore both of them.

There are salient exceptions of course, as will be mentioned later, but all too common is the case where social justice activists cynically accuse their less socially active brothers and sisters of excessively privatizing the Gospel; of confusing love with sentiment, with being nice; of neglecting Jesus' non-negotiable demand that we side with the poor; and of identifying Christian practice simply with churchgoing, with private prayer and private morality, especially sexual morality.

Why, this group asks, are those not actively involved with social justice forever talking about sexual morality and *Humanae Vitae*, and never about the social encyclicals? Why are people so fanatical about abortion and then so calloused regarding poverty, women's rights, immigration and capital punishment?

Those less active in social justice return the accusations. All too common is the angry and judgmental accusation that those most active in social justice no longer pray; that they have the Gospel confused with Greenpeace; that they neglect the fact that Jesus' non-negotiable demands radically invade one's private world and are equally as demanding there, in the order of sexual morality and private charity, as they are in the area of social justice; and that talk of justice and equality for all is hopelessly compromised when it issues from hearts hardened to the unborn.

I think Kasemann's words are true here. The liberals are not pious and the pious are not liberal.

This is a bad situation. If we are to offer any kind of help to a world which is interested neither in social justice nor in contemplation, a world which, effectively, has written us off, then we had best become liberal and pious, contemplative and socially active, both at once.

In my opinion there is nothing more urgent on the Christian agenda than this question, the marriage between social justice and contemplation. Both sides on this issue have correctly sensed that survival is what is at stake.

Unless the issues surrounding justice, poverty, war, the

ecology, ethnic rights and women's rights are addressed we won't have a world within which to practice our piety. Conversely if private prayer, private morality, and contemplation die, then we will still somehow lose the world or, certainly, we will lose any world worth living in.

The signs of the times need to be read: Vatican II, the recovery of the social Gospel, the growing affluence of First World Christians, the breakdown of marriage and family life, the ecological crisis, the rise of feminism, the threat of nuclear war, oppressive injustice in the Third World and the shrinking size of our planet have conspired to make it vital, a matter of life and death, that we make a marriage between social justice and contemplation. If we do not, we have no future.

As mentioned earlier, some have etched out a path toward this: Catherine Doherty and the Madonna House Apostolate, Richard Rohr and the Centre for Action and Contemplation, Jim Wallis and Sojourners, Jean Vanier and L'Arche, Sheila Cassidy and the Hospice movement, Gustavo Gutierrez with his brand of Liberation Theology which always puts justice, love and grace together in the same breath, and, of course, John Paul II and many bishops' conferences with their social encyclicals and pastoral letters on justice.

Others, including Mother Teresa, Henri Nouwen, Dorothy Day, Thomas Merton, and Dan Berrigan began this work decades ago.

In these we see the beginnings of a path, some charting of the uncharted. Action and contemplation, private morality and social awareness, prophetic anger and understanding, liberalness and piety, are being married. From their lead we should take our cue.

Make Your Welcome Hearty

IN OCTOBER 1933 Peter Maurin wrote the following poem
and commentary in the *Catholic Worker*:

> People who are in need
>   and are not afraid to beg
>   give to people not in need
> the occasion to do good
>   for goodness sake.
>
> Modern society calls the beggar
>   bum and panhandler
>   and gives him the bum's rush.
> But the Greeks used to say
>   that people in need
>   are ambassadors of the gods.
>
> Although you may be called
>   bums and panhandlers
>   you are in fact the ambassadors of God.
> As God's ambassadors
>   you should be given
>   food, clothing and shelter
> by those who are able to give it.
>
> Mohammedan teachers tell us
>   that God commands hospitality

and hospitality is still practised
   in Mohammedan countries.
But the duty of hospitality
   is neither taught nor practised
   in Christian countries.

The poor are no longer
   fed, clothed and sheltered
   at personal sacrifice
but at the expense of the taxpayers.

And because the poor
   are no longer
   fed, clothed and sheltered
   at personal sacrifice
the pagans say about Christians,
   "See how they pass the buck."

Maurin goes on to comment that a church council of the fifth
century obliged bishops to establish houses of hospitality in
connection with every parish. These houses were open to the
poor, the sick, the orphaned, the aged and the needy of every
kind. The idea was that one must always be ready to recognize Christ in the unfamiliar face and so every parish and
every home was to have its "Christ room," set aside to receive the ambassadors of God who appear in the form of the
needy and the visiting.

Hebrews 13:2 asks us not to neglect hospitality, remark-
ing that, in receiving strangers "some have entertained angels
without knowing it."

Lately we have neglected hospitality. There has been a
bad slippage. No longer in our parishes, homes and hearts is

there a "Christ room." Not only do we no longer see hospitality as a privilege, we no longer see it even as duty.

There are a number of reasons for the demise of our sense of hospitality. One of them, surely, is the one Maurin points out, we have turned the duty of hospitality over to government agencies, the taxpayer, social security, social services. They are asked to take care of the widow, the orphan, the aged and the stranger.

More important, though, the demise of hospitality has occurred because we have developed a sense of privacy and efficiency that militate against it.

Our culture is becoming ever more narcissistic and idiosyncratic, that is, more and more we have the attitude that things are our own. We speak of my space, my time, my family, my home, my community, my room, my stereo, my plans, my agenda, my friendships, my effectiveness, and even, in a way, of my church.

In such a context we allow other persons into our lives, our homes, our communities and our churches, most selectively. We are hospitable to our own, to those who meet our standards and our timetables. This invariably excludes the poor from our hearts, homes and churches, since they have no sense of our standards and timetables. Their problems are neither antiseptic nor conveniently scheduled.

Compounding this is the problem of efficiency. Thomas Merton, asked what he thought the worst problem was facing Western civilization, instead of answering with something like "injustice," "moral decay" or "lack of interiority," replied simply, "Efficiency!"

Our problem in the Western world, everywhere from the Pentagon to our monasteries, is that the plant must run! The classes must be taught, the crops must be sown and harvested, the kids need to be driven for their lessons, the meeting must run as scheduled, the supper must be cooked, the essay needs to be written, the mortgage needs to be paid, the plane needs to be caught, things must keep running, there is no other way, the show must go on, we need to do what we need to do!

In all that, partly, we are losing our souls because in it there is no space or time for hospitality and hospitality is the mark of a truly gracious soul.

Would that the hallmark of our Christian homes and churches be the graciousness of our welcome and would that, when we die, each of us might be most remembered for that, our hospitality, the graciousness of our welcome!

It's Easy to Sacrifice Others

"IT IS BETTER that one man should die for the people."

Why does that line have so haunting a sound? Why does it sound like the refrain of a litany? It haunts, not because of any particular poetic merit, but because it expresses a perverse truth that invariably fascinates. In a caption it rationalizes death, deals death, and justifies it.

Caiphas, the high priest, first used this phrase to justify Christ's death. Christ's person and message were upsetting things, upsetting the way life had been, upsetting a delicate balance of inter-relationships that had built up, like a complex ecology, over many years.

Caiphas and the other leaders at that time did not in fact have a lot of personal things against Christ. They were just scared. There was more fear than malevolence present when Christ was condemned. It was fear that prompted Caiphas to utter this phrase and so justify his acquiescence to an innocent death.

That fear, and that phrase, have always been the great rationalization for death and have justified our acquiescence to countless deaths; so much so that it is possible to construct a litany for death with this phrase as its refrain:

- When we favor capital punishment and support the idea that some persons, irrespective of what kind of lives they are leading, should be put to death, we are saying: better that one person should die for the people.

- When there is abortion, when an unborn child's life is taken, our society is saying: better that one person should die for the people.
- When we refuse to care properly for the poor in our society, when we say we cannot afford welfare, Medicare, day care, free education and the support of mothers at home with small children, when we let the poor fall through the cracks rather than upset our standard of living, we are saying: better that one person should die for the people.
- When someone is slandered in conversation and we, because of fear, say nothing, we are saying: better that one person should die for the people.
- When our countries bomb their neighbors to insure their own security, when our countries use unjustifiable amounts of money, talent and resources to build up weapons of defense, we are saying: better that one person should die for the people.
- When our countries do not take in refugees because we fear that they will take some of our jobs and have an adverse effect on our standard of living, we are saying: better that one person should die for the people.
- When our countries refuse to admit that so much of the discontent and terrorism of our age is the natural by-product of a way of life, a system, wherein the rich benefit from the poor, when we do nothing about this because it would mean some very upsetting changes, we are saying: better that one person should die for the people.
- When, because of the pressures of our lifestyles, we draw too excessively upon the world's resources, when, for the same reason, we cannot properly respect nature and by

exorbitant consumption and its concomitant pollution we destroy the environment for future generations, we are saying: better that one person should die for the people.

- When a youth gang in Montreal brutally murders a homosexual man with AIDS on a subway, both the aggressors and the bystanders (for different reasons) are saying: better that one person should die for the people.
- When Martin Luther King, Malcolm X, Oscar Romero, Jerzy Popieluszko, Stan Rather, Michael Rodrigo, and Anne Frank are killed, when the KKK murder three civil rights workers in Mississippi in the early 1960s, when oppressive regimes around the world intimidate people and make them disappear, someone is saying: better that one person should die for the people.

Death's great litany echoing through the centuries, from Caiphas to us—better that one person should die for the people, better this death than that our lives should be so upset, better this than that we should have to change!

Cardinal Jaime Sin of the Philippines once commented upon the place of courage within the spectrum of virtue:

> Strength without compassion is violence
> Compassion without justice is sentiment
> Justice without love is Marxism
> And . . . love without justice is baloney!

We all need greater courage. We need to pray for that. We need to pray to be less intimidated by our own weaknesses and fears, to be more courageous in moving beyond the comforts of affluence, privilege and good name, to be less timid, less small, less petty and more willing to sacrifice and perhaps even to die rather than to acquiesce to the death of an innocent person by uttering, however unreflectively and unconsciously, the phrase: better that one person should die for the people.

Alive with Prophetic Pain

I HAD A LENGTHY TALK with a friend of mine who is a Catholic feminist. Articulate and not afraid to express her anger, she talked openly about her pain. She is frustrated with inequality in the church, frustrated that she can never be ordained. The tears flowed freely, she wanted to leave the church she had grown up in, but something held her back.

A day later, quite by chance, I was doing a marriage interview and the young woman about to be married spoke tearfully about the same pain. She too was considering leaving the church.

In telling their stories, both commented that what was really pushing them to leave the church was the pain they experienced while attending the Eucharist. Both filled with pain, anger and bitterness and were reduced to tears.

Superficially, one might conclude that their pain is most acute at Eucharist because a male presides there. This however, I submit, is a secondary explanation. Their pain touches on something deeper, that must send a signal to the whole church. Irrespective of the fact that it is mixed with other pains, they are experiencing the pain of the prophet.

Scripture states that *prophets die somewhere between the altar and sanctuary*. Given that, should it be so surprising that people will experience their deepest pains at liturgy? Given too that the church had best be looking at and listening to those who feel killed at Eucharist, namely those who have to die a little to stand in the sanctuary, for the sake of the church and its health we had best embrace those persons and this pain. And we had better tell those persons how important it is that they do not leave us.

Both women were convinced that this kind of pain at Eucharist indicates that it is best that they should leave.

However their pain is prophetic. It indicates that something is amiss, but amiss with the whole body, not with one individual.

Their pain also indicates that the Eucharist in fact is effective. By its very nature it is meant to be a place of anguish as well as a place of celebration. The Eucharist is meant to break us open, to break us down, to grind and transubstantiate us into one community of love.

Since we come to Eucharist far from united, each of us trapped in his or her own narcissism and selfishnesses, we need to be broken down before unity and community can take place. This does not happen without pain and anguish.

However it is not necessarily those who feel the most anguish who most need to be broken down or changed. Their pain indicates that there is something wrong in the body.

I am heartened in the faith, even if not delighted emotionally, when I hear of somebody who fills with anguish at Eucharist. It means that she or he is sincere, that she or he has deep roots within the Eucharistic community, and that the Eucharist is still working.

And these, the ones who fill with pain, need to be specially embraced and listened to. Those who feel oppressed, excluded and who die (in whatever way) in the sanctuary are most often the prophetic voices even if they themselves are inarticulate. Their pain is not.

Karl Barth stated that in the incarnation God descends, moving from "height to the depth, from victory to defeat, from riches to poverty, from triumph to suffering, from life to death." In those who suffer, God is revealed—and this is nowhere more true than at the Eucharist.

Pain is a word. Like God's spirit it gives expression to what is too deep for words. Pain, accepted without final bitterness and persevered in, is prophecy. It is God's voice in a calloused church and world. It comes from conscience and speaks to conscience.

In the Eucharist, among other things, the passion and death of Christ are being re-enacted. Obviously those who are suffering the most and are doing some dying are the Christ figures.

That is why it is so important that those who feel like these women, those who fill with pain and tears at the Eucharist, remain in the church and remain at the Eucharist. Without prophetic tears, we grow ever more deaf.

And prophets die somewhere between altar and sanctuary. But their groan is a word, a voice, that cannot be killed.

11

READING THE SIGNS OF THE TIMES: KEEPING ONE'S BALANCE IN A COMPLEX WORLD

There is no short cut, no patent tram-road, to wisdom. After all the centuries of invention, the soul's path lies through the thorny wilderness which must be still trodden in solitude, with bleeding feet, with sobs for help, as it was trodden by them of old time.

(George Eliot)

Keep Your Faith in Balance

I SHARE WITH YOU here four tales of imbalance. Each is the story of a person who is sincere, Christian and dedicated, but has fallen from wholeness. From these stories of imbalance, hopefully, we will be able to see where proportion lies.

A TALE OF THE NEGLECT OF SOCIAL JUSTICE

A bishop I know recounts this story. One day he received a phone call from an angry lady:

"Why," she demanded, "are you and the other bishops so hung up on social justice? Why don't you stick with what the church is all about, liturgy, prayer and morality?"

He answered her with another question, "What would you do, if you were a bishop and someone called you and said: 'Our parish priest refuses to preach about private prayer and private morality. He tells us that these are fads that a few contemplatives have started. They are not important in the Christian life'?"

"I would suspend the man on the spot!" was her reply.

"Then," replied the bishop, "what am I to do with a person who phones and says: 'Our priest refuses to preach social justice. He tells us that this is just a fad started by the liberation theologians and a few social-justice types. You can be a good Christian and never practice social justice'?"

This lady's question betrays a dangerous imbalance.

Spirituality is reduced to prayer and private morality. As important as these are, they are not enough.

A TALE OF THE NEGLECT OF PRAYER AND PRIVATE MORALITY

Some years back while doing graduate work, I was working as a chaplain at a hostel in a poorer section of San Francisco. One of the persons I was working with, a very dedicated person, said to me:

"Father, do you really think God gives a damn whether you say your morning and evening prayers, whether you hold a grudge, or whether you hop in and out of bed a few times with someone you aren't married to? These small, private things are so unimportant.

"What possible difference do they make in the light of the larger questions of peace and justice? God hasn't got time for our private little prayers and little moral struggles!"

For him spirituality meant the struggle for peace and justice, the taking care of God's poor. Just that. Private prayer and private morality were so dwarfed by these larger issues as to seem unimportant.

As important as is the struggle for peace and justice, being a prophet implies more.

A TALE OF THE NEGLECT OF JOY AND CELEBRATION

I attended an international conference in Belgium on local church, which brought together people from all parts of the world. On the second-to-last day the organizers called a halt to work, to all the discussing and theologizing. We were all sent off to the beautiful city of Bruges for tours, cocktails, dining and celebrating.

In my own group was a young nun from the Third World. There was no doubt that she was a woman who prayed, whose private morals were beyond suspicion, and that her whole life was being lived for the poor. But she struggled, and deeply, to be joyful, to celebrate and not to be angry and bitter. She found our half-day celebration a tough chore, an evil to be endured, a waste of time and an insult to the poor.

Again, I submit, there is here an imbalance. What is lacking from this lady's life? Certainly not prayer, private morality or a preferential option for the poor.

What is lacking is friendship, celebration and the greatest asceticism of all, that of being a joyful, celebrating and non-bitter person. Prophetic witness lies as much in being a happy and non-bitter person as in being a person of prayer, morality and social justice; though admittedly the former is based a lot on the latter.

A TALE OF THE NEGLECT OF LOVE

After delivering a talk on prophecy, a lady challenged me.

"You spoke too little about anger! You were too soft. Prophecy is all about challenge, anger and righteousness. Without a proper anger, you cannot be prophetic!"

She said more, mostly about the need for anger and a bitter challenge to the mainstream culture.

Again, at least in her challenge to me, there was imbalance. She spoke constantly of anger, of challenge, of criticalness. Never once did she mention love. Her attitude toward the culture was that of disdain, bitterness, anger and disgust.

Nowhere in her did I detect compassion, sadness, sympathy or love toward or about, those she was supposedly preaching to.

A prophet, as Jim Wallis suggests, is always characterized more by love than by anger. Likewise, as psychology points out, we can only truly challenge another to change if that other first feels loved by us.

There are certain nonnegotiable prongs within Christian spirituality, namely prayer and private morality, a commitment to justice and peace, the discipline of joy and celebration (that is, the Christian duty to be a happy person), and the duty to challenge by love.

And the key to health is proportion.

Listening to Different Voices

I AM particularly fond of biography. Stories of people's lives, save for the cheaper accounts of the lives of the rich and famous, are a special kind of literature. A good story throws light on everyone's life since, as Willa Cather says, "there are only two or three human stories, and they go on repeating themselves as fiercely as if they had never happened."

This is even more true when we are dealing with the story of someone of our own generation, who, even though his or her life may be different from ours, has felt the changes of the world at the same time as we did. There is a certain affinity, compassion, con-naturality, and even a mysticism, that exists among those who experience the same things at roughly the same time.

Where were you when Kennedy was shot? Do you remember the cold war, the fall-out shelters, the advent of Presley, the Beatles, hard rock, hard drugs, Woodstock, the Vietnam war, the world going crazy in 1968?

Do you remember the time before the sexual revolution, Vatican II, the slide of marriage and family life, the hopeless fragmentation of knowledge, and the anger, polarization, and yuppyism of the 1980s?

These events were the acid, we are the litmus paper. Most of us, I suspect, turned the same colors.

Given that affinity among us, I want to share part of my own story. Not because it is in any way extraordinary, but precisely because it is so ordinary and typical. I want to de-

scribe some of the colors I have turned and am still turning.
Perhaps it will be helpful to you in dealing with your own
story since we share a common place in history. We have
been dropped in the same test tube.

I am a child of our age and, for this reason, straddle two
cultures and am subject to two voices. The earliest voice that
spoke to me was that of my parents and of their culture.
They were immigrants, economically poor, pious, Christian.
So was their culture.

Their voice spoke as follows. Worldly success is not important. What is important are Christ, family, church. Duty
and self-sacrifice are more important than personal fulfillment. Life here in this world is not so important. We can live
in dissatisfaction and frustration since, before death, we live
as in a valley of tears, in a world in which the symphony can
never be finished. Ecstasy must be postponed until the next
life. Personal morality, especially if it has to do with sex, is a
big deal. So too is private prayer. You should be charitable to
the poor. (There was little talk of social justice since we were
in fact the poor.) The world is a cold and pagan place, set
over against the church. The voice said: be suspicious, always suspicious, of the world and its ways.

But already as a child another voice and another culture
began to seep in. I read magazines, listened to the radio,
watched TV and movies, looked at catalogues and travel
brochures, and began to read a literature which spoke in another voice. Each year too I watched events irrevocably
changing our lives and our culture.

This new voice spoke as follows. You are poor now, but
you can move from rags to riches. You were born the immigrant, but you can live as something else. Family, church and
Christ are important, but so too is success, a career. Make

something of yourself. Be admired. Duty and sacrifice need sometimes to be jettisoned for personal fulfillment; after all, you only live the once and there is meant to be some life after birth (as well as after death). Private prayer and private morality, including sexual ethics, are not such a big deal. Do not be suspicious of the world. It often affirms life where the church does not. Be suspicious instead of the church and its hangups, timidities and fears. Look at where it blocks life.

I have spent most of my life caught between these two voices—confused, stretched, unsure, torn, testing one, then the other.

One of these voices, that of my parents, has won an essential victory. But that victory is still bitterly contested and is far from complete and unequivocal.

Parts of me belong to the culture that was not my parents' and these sometimes win their own kind of victory. Moreover in head and heart it is not so clear that that one voice, my parents', is everywhere identifiable with Christ's voice and that the other voice is always identifiable with the world.

My parents' culture had its faults. It could be racist, bigoted, prejudiced, narrow, timid and unhealthily fearful. Invariably there was the timidity of the immigrant, the bias of the ghetto, "us against them," "stay with your own kind," "don't even selectively try to love what's outside."

As well, the other voice, despite its obvious bias for the world, speaks of a universalism, an openness, and a challenge beyond fear and timidity that echoes the Gospel better than the former voice.

So where does that leave me?

Living a question. Uncertain of a lot of things. Steady in some convictions, gasping for oxygen in others. Convinced that old-time religion and fundamentalism are not the answer, but suspicious that perhaps I, we, somehow need to be inner immigrants.

Beyond those questions, though, is a growing comfort, totally undeserved, to be sure, in a surer knowledge that we are loved by God, myself no less than everyone else.

Given that comfort, I feel no panic about the two voices. Being pulled between them is quite an adventure.

Being Normal Is Not Our Goal

IN AN INTERVIEW in the *National Catholic Reporter*, Richard McBrien suggests that the Roman Catholic Church ought to change its law regarding priestly celibacy. His argument is as straightforward as it is convincing: "I mean, healthy people are sexually active people. That's normal. So why do we make priests behave as if they're not healthy and normal?" (January 20th, 1989)

The functions and dysfunctions of priestly celibacy might be debated, as might McBrien's argument. What has implications in that statement for issues far beyond clerical celibacy is the appeal to normalcy as the criterion for health and rightness, "That's normal. So why are we acting otherwise?"

That is very persuasive and powerful. What is healthy is normal. To deviate from that imperative is to risk sickness. One must act as normal people do.

There is much truth in that. There are serious risks in thinking one can be healthy and yet live differently than normal persons.

The proof of the pudding is in the eating, and, as McBrien goes on to point out, celibacy does in fact take its toll upon the lives of many priests who end up unhealthy— succumbing to alcohol, a rationalized double life, gadgetry, compensating consumption or repressed sexuality that frequently then manifests itself in the abuse of power.

What is true here for celibacy is also true for many other areas wherein religion, or anything else, ask one to live what most others are not living. For example, in monasticism (as well as more recently in social justice circles) one sees a dark side among some—weirdness, repression of need, élitist self-righteousness, neuroses and anger paraded as sanctity, and, as in clerical celibacy gone sour, the misuse of power.

One takes a very serious risk in not letting what is more normal adjudicate health.

However, with that being admitted, Goethe might aptly be quoted: "The risks of life are many, and safety lies among them." The Gospel asks of us risk, to put out into the deep waters. This demand, if followed, will precisely displace us from what we would like to live as normal life. Let me explain.

The word church comes from the word ecclesia, from the Greek, *ek kaleo* (*ek*—out of; *kaleo*—to call). To be a member of the church is to be called out of something.

What are we called out of? Precisely, normal life, as unchallenged human propensity would like to define it.

Outside of a challenge from something beyond us we automatically identify what is normal with what most people are living at a given time. Normalcy by popular consensus. Health and sanctity defined by Gallup poll.

When this happens then invariably normalcy identifies itself with idiosyncratic preference, the good life: a good job, a good romance, a good house, good vacations, good sex, a good body and enough money, freedom and leisure to enjoy it all. That is what all of us normal people in fact want.

Baptism into Christian life is meant to be a displacement from that. It is meant, precisely, to call us out of that normalcy. It is meant to derail us, to put a belt around us and lead us where we would rather not go.

Entry into church is, to use an older phrase, a consecration. That word too, like church, means displacement, derailment.

For most of us the word consecration is a pious, sacristy word. It speaks of consecrated chalices, altars, churches. Of itself, that is not an improper use of the word. To consecrate something is to displace it from normal use: an ordinary cup is set aside to become a chalice, an ordinary table is set aside to become an altar, or an ordinary building is set aside to become a church.

However when we think of consecration in that sense it generally takes on such connotations of piety and separateness that it means little to us in ordinary life.

Let me attempt another way of explaining this: To be consecrated is to be displaced from normalcy.

Imagine yourself setting out on holiday. You have planned your trip in detail and are eagerly looking forward to enjoying this well-deserved rest. You pack the car and go. On the way you come upon a serious traffic accident. Some people are hurt and dying. There is no one else around. At that moment you become consecrated. Your holiday plans must be, for the moment, set aside, displaced, with the rest of normal life. A very legitimate agenda must be set aside.

Christian life displaces in the same way. It sets aside what we would, without baptism, define as normal life.

A friend of mine who is deeply committed to family, church and social issues is, when overwhelmed and frustrated, fond of saying, "If there is reincarnation in my next life, I am coming back as a yuppie. I'll have nothing to do with having kids, church, or the poor. I'll have season tickets to everything, go on a lot of ski trips and let God take care of his own world."

There is as much wisdom as self-pity in that remark. It

speaks of a genuine baptism, of a life that has been consecrated in that the needs of the kindgom have derailed plans
for a more selfish fulfillment.

The human instinct is to define the normal by idiosyncratic preference and social consensus. We need to challenge
this if religion is to have an agenda that includes celibacy, social justice or anything else which goes against what most
people are in fact living.

High Season for Religion Foes

THESE ARE TOUGH DAYS for those who believe in the institutional church and in organized religion. Daily our news documents incidents of sin, corruption, abused power, misguided fanaticism and betrayed trust—all done in the name of religion or under its guise!

Pedophilia among Roman Catholic priests, sex and money scandals among TV evangelists, hostage-taking and bombings by fundamentalist Arabs, Irish Catholics and Hindu Sikhs, these and other lesser scandals fill the front pages. As one commentator put it, "this is the church's Watergate!"

Many people's faith is shaken; understandably so. Trust, once given then betrayed, is not easily restored. Faith in organized religion is difficult at the best of times and so, given all this disillusionment, it is becoming ever easier for people to believe that they would best go through life independent of the institutional church.

Moreover for those who despise or ignore organized religion (cultured agnostics, religious lone-rangers, anti-clericals) this is high season.

What all these scandals are doing is helping confirm their most hopeful suspicions. Religion is a hoax; organized church practice serves the interests of those who organize it; Roman Catholic celibacy is a front; everyone has an angle; in the church, as elsewhere, sex and money are what it's ultimately all about: the institutional part of religion is what corrupts faith; pure self-sacrifice does not exist within the churches;

one is best off without organized religion; Jesus founded a kingdom, humans created the churches. All these Watergate-type revelations are finally revealing the truth!

What is to be said and done in the face of all of this?

All healing begins with a lancing of the wound. We should, despite the pain and humiliation of all of this, be grateful that the truth is being exposed. In the long run the truth will set us free.

In the short run the prognosis is less positive. We have to be prepared for a season, perhaps a very long one, of continued pain and embarrassment and a further erosion of trust. We have to accept this and accept it without self-pity, rationalization, half-baked justifications, or any attempts to water down the seriousness of what is revealed in these scandals. Partly we are sick and, like a virus that has infected the body, this has to run its course and the body, in pain and fever, has to build up a new immune system. In the short run we can only do what Lamentations advises: "Put your mouth to the dust and wait!"

Beyond that, those of us who are not directly involved in these scandals, either personally or institutionally, must resist the temptation to distance ourselves and our churches from them with the attitude, "Don't look at me, I'm innocent, this is somebody else's problem!"

It is our problem, irrespective of whether we are innocent or guilty. All Christians, along with all other sincere believers, form one body. Christ's body. We are all in this together, with Christ. We may not facilely link ourselves with our church's graced moments, its saints, martyrs, and proud achievements, and then slickly distance ourselves from its dark history, its compromises, its perverseness, its pedophilia and its sex and money scandals. To be a member of the church, to be a believer, is to be linked to all of this, grace and sin.

In this context it is significant to point out that Christ died between two thieves. He was innocent; they were not. However, because his sacrifice was seen against that horizon, it was judged by association, by those present, to be as tainted as the deaths of those he died with. People watching the crucifixion did not distinguish between who was guilty and who was innocent. They assessed what they saw en bloc. For them all crucifixions meant the same thing.

The church is still judged in the same way. To be a church member is still to be connected, by association, with sin and sinners. Christ was the object of suspicion and misunderstanding. Every kind of accusation was leveled against him. This will be true, always, of his church.

Like him, the church will always be seen by outsiders as framed against a certain horizon—on display with scoundrels, child molesters, fakes, frauds, bad thieves and good thieves. The crucifixion of Christ is still going on and it is mixed in with the personal tragedies of honest and dishonest sinners. Christ is always pinned up among thieves.

But the church need offer no particular apologetics for this. The historical Jesus was found there. Why should the church not be found there?

As the great Protestant theologian Friedrich Schleiermacher stated, already a century ago, in *Speeches to the Cultured Despisers of Religion* (n.e. 1958), the temptation is always to despise religion in its positive form, namely in its concrete historical expression in the churches where it finds itself hopelessly and inextricably intertwined with the sin, pettiness and foibles of ordinary human beings. Invariably the temptation is to say "I can handle God, but I won't be involved with all this human mess we call the church!"

To speak that line is to utter the greatest ecclesial heresy there is. To speak it is also to abandon the true Christ for an idol. Jesus walked with sinners, ate with them, was accused with them and died with them. The church is true when it is in solidarity with him, especially in that. Lately the church has been dying a lot with sinners. It has been a humiliating experience—but then, so was the crucifixion!

Abortion: No Quick Solutions

FOR MORE AND MORE OF US, I suspect, the issue of abortion brings up feelings of helplessness that border on despair. The issue is so important that a conscientious person may not remain silent for long without incurring guilt.

But what responses are truly productive? What can genuinely help change this situation? What would Jesus do? Would he organize political lobbies? Lobby for pro-life candidates? Withhold portions of his income tax? Demonstrate outside abortion clinics? Chain himself to a fence?

I honestly do not know. There is in me neither the vision nor the will to try to answer those questions. What I do want to offer, and rather hesitantly at that, are the rather meager fruits from my own struggles with these questions. I have always been, and remain, uncompromisingly pro-life. Rightly or wrongly, however, I have not always been involved in the active struggle, the political organizing and the demonstrations. Why?

Sometimes I rationalize that if God had wanted me to be a prophet he would have given me greater strength and a less ambiguous vision. As it is I am Germanic, complete with the proclivity for procrastination and the need for the infallible assurance, before I act, that I am not making a mistake. But, these things aside, my hesitation has also been based upon a belief that this issue, for all its urgency, has no quick solution.

To begin to explain this, I need to speak about power. What kind of power may we seize upon to try to change this situation? Too many people, I am afraid, have placed their hopes in legal power, political power. The belief is that if we work hard enough we can get the laws changed, put abortionists on trial, close down abortion clinics. To this end we demonstrate, withhold taxes, organize lobbies and chain ourselves to fences. I am not suggesting that these things do not need to be done; after all, real people are dying. This battle is more than academic.

And yet the only real solution is long-range. This battle, in the end, cannot be won legally and politically. Ultimately, more than laws, hearts need to be changed. Conversion is the only effective way of ultimately ending abortions. Abortion clinics will shut down when nobody shows up at their doors any more.

To win the battle politically, without a conversion of hearts, will simply roll back the clock, drive people into illegal backroom clinics, allow abortionists like Henry Morgentaler to posture as martyrs, and lead to a renewed effort on the part of the pro-abortionists. It will be a temporary slowing down of abortions, at best.

Moreover this conversion must involve a conversion within relationships. Today the issue of abortion cannot be fairly thought out because radical feminism has claimed pro-choice as one of its key liberation items. To be pro-life is to be classified as anti-feminist.

This is tragic for both sides on this issue because, consequently, sincere men and women are forced to distance themselves from feminism; and feminists, on their part, are all too often forced to distance themselves from one of the things they would most need to change in order to bring about healthier relationships between women and men, namely the stopping of abortion.

Radical feminism has seen, and rightly so, a connection between the abortion issue and feminine oppression. Unfortunately it has not always, in my opinion, understood that connection correctly, even as it intuited its gravity. The oppression of women in our culture is especially sexual. In a culture which is sexually irresponsible the inevitable losers are women. They end up suffering the most.

When a culture exists within which men and women do not trust each other, within which sexual irresponsibility is encouraged in (and even, at times, forced upon) young people, and within which women—for reasons which are often far beyond their free choosing—sleep with and conceive children from men they hardly know, you inevitably have abortion.

But it is not the girl or woman who shows up at the abortion clinic who is most to blame, nor perhaps even the boy or man who impregnates her. We are all to blame. The lady who stands before the abortionists is, with her child, victim, the tip of a pine cone of irresponsibility and oppression. And, on her part, abortion is an act of resignation. No woman ever really wants an abortion and no woman is ever happy for having had one.

As Ginny Soley puts it:

Abortion is, finally, an act of despair. The decision to have an abortion reflects a woman's lack of confidence in herself. It means that she does not trust the man with whom she is in relationship. It means that she has no belief in long-lasting, long-term, stable relationships between men and women. In fact it means that she has lost confidence in life itself. (*Sojourners*, October 1986)

The road to final victory on the issue of abortion is long, the task mammoth. Hearts need to change, relationships need to change, sexual patterns need to change, oppression needs to be recognized; and real villains and real victims must be more accurately named.

Pro-life and Anti-abortion

THE NEXT FEW YEARS will be decisive regarding the question of abortion. The battle will be definitely lost or won.

Bottom line, we have had, in the Western world, abortion on demand for decades. However, this has never sat easy. There has been, even as the movement ploughed irresistibly and seemingly irrevocably forward, a massive growth of resistance. That resistance has ripened just at a time when governments, for a variety of reasons, are being forced to re-examine the laws that have given us abortion on demand.

During the next few years, certainly in North America, new laws will be brought in or old laws will be upheld which will, I fear, cement the issue into one mold or the other for a long time to come. Consequently the time is critical for pro-life. People tend to accept as OK whatever they have got used to. Practice becomes custom, custom becomes law, legality is seen as morality. Our culture is used to abortion on demand. The longer this persists the more irrevocable it becomes.

Given this situation and the present political state, there is a chance, a last chance perhaps for a long time, to again instill in our political system the will to protect the unborn. But we must act quickly and massively.

Many of us are not used to acting regarding this question. We are pro-life, but in a rather antiseptic way. Pro-life is part of our curriculum vitae: we are officially pro-life; we offer it moral support; we write articles and make statements about its place within the wider spectrum of social justice; but we are entirely absent from the picket lines and from any direct lobbying or confrontational process.

I have been an antiseptic pro-lifer. I have written an article a year against abortion, spoken out against it in my classrooms, and even addressed pro-life groups, but I have not walked a picket line, written or phoned a Member of Parliament or realistically confronted anyone on this issue for fifteen years. Given this background, I was deeply cut, as one is when a truly prophetic word is heard, by an editorial, "An open letter to socially concerned Catholics: resist abortion now!" in *Catholic New Times*, June 25th, 1988.

Since there are out there, I suspect, many other antiseptic pro-lifers like myself, I share with you, by way of a brief précis, some of the salient points of that very prophetic editorial.

One of the most unfortunate developments within the church and within society at large is the phenomenon wherein both conservative and liberal Christians tend to lack a consistent approach to pro-life.

Liberals, while clamoring loudly for social justice in the areas of economics, racial and sexual discrimination, immigration laws, housing and Third World concerns, have been simply tolerant of and silent about abortion.

Conservatives, on the other hand, have championed the fight against abortion, but have frequently reduced the concern for life to a simple anti-abortion focus. Thus, while speaking clearly in favor of life on one front, they have been noisily in favor of capital punishment, nuclear arms and the system of liberal capitalism (which sees society as a system of competing individual rights which must be legally bartered).

As well, they have been less fully for life in their views regarding women.

However, with that said, the editorial goes on to praise the conservatives' pro-life efforts. Pro-life groups, despite being single-issue focused and inconsistent in the support of life, have nonetheless "borne the political heat of the day on the issues of abortion. And they have borne it with courage." Their passion is a welcome challenge.

Tolerant liberals, who often find pro-life tactics distasteful, would do well to examine themselves and see whether they are backing off from the abortion issue because of the current sense of what is socially acceptable.

The editorial goes on to say that the social virtues of tolerance may never be invoked "to legitimate the decertifications of the unborn as human beings." The work of justice, it asserts, is "totally lacking in integrity if, by omission or commission, we participate in the bartering away of the rights of the smallest and weakest members of our society."

Moreover we may not believe "that the rights of a woman, or of any other group, will be served as long as the rights of one group, the unborn, can be negotiated out of existence. A society which assumes the divine right of deciding when life begins will all too easily move on to decide when it should end and for whom."

Such a clear stand on abortion does not, the article rightly asserts, diminish the sincerity and admirable social commitment of many pro-choice persons. Nor does it withhold compassion for or judge those who have had abortions. It simply offers a consistent ethic for life and, prophetically, stands up for those who have the least voice. Finally and importantly, it calls upon all of us antiseptic pro-lifers to do something, actually to act:

In the name of God, do something. Go to the phone and call your Member of Parliament. Walk a picket line. Commit civil disobedience. Wear a button. Start or join an action group. This is politics and pressure is now what counts. Pressure the Members of Parliament. May they not rest in peace!

12

DEATH WASHES CLEAN: THE COMMUNION OF SAINTS

I am not sure this planet is home. Do you ever have the feeling you're a tourist on earth? You'll be walking down the street and suddenly it's like a moving postcard around you . . . I'm a tourist on earth . . . They have funny customs here, but I am fond of the place. When I remind myself I am a tourist, when I do that, I can almost recall what it's like where I came from. There's a magnet that's pulling us, pulling us against the fence of this world's limits. I have this strange feeling that we come from the other side of the fence.

(RICHARD BACH)

Death Washes Things Clean

WHEN I WAS A CHILD, as part of our family prayer we used to pray for a happy death.

In my young mind I spontaneously associated a happy death with dying cradled in the loving arms of family and church, fully at peace with God and everyone around you.

Not many, even very good persons, die like that. Given the randomness and contingencies of human circumstances, very often people die in broken and compromised situations: bitter, unforgiving and unforgiven, not having dealt with their own sins, unreconciled with their own families and the church, alienated, indifferent to God and community, angry, drunk, dead by drug overdose, by suicide. Or at times death catches people before they have had or taken the time to say things that should have been said or done things that should have been done. Very often when people die they leave behind, on this side of heaven, much unfinished business. As an old confiteor has it, there is need to be reconciled for what has been said and left unsaid, done and left undone.

To cite a few small examples: counseling a man in his fifties who was unable to forgive himself because his mother (when he was seven and unaware that she was dying) had asked him to come and hug her and he, inhibited, male, had refused. More than forty years later there was still some unfinished business.

In another case, I officiated at the funeral of a man who, just before getting killed in an accident, had had a major blowup with his family and stomped out of the house in a rage of anger.

Many of us, I am sure, have had persons close to us die with whom we had unfinished business. Perhaps we hurt them or they hurt us and it was never reconciled; or we should have given them more of ourselves but were too pre-occupied with our own lives to reach out at the time; or we hated them and should have made some gesture of reconcili-ation and now it is too late! Death has separated them from us and what was left unfinished now lies irrevocably unfin-ished, and we live with guilt and keep saying "If only, if only . . ."

These "if onlys" will disappear if we take seriously the Christian doctrine concerning the communion of saints. This doctrine, so central to our faith that it is one of the doctrines enshrined in the creed, asks us to believe that we are still in vital communion with those who have died, indeed in privi-leged communication.

To believe in the communion of saints is to believe that those who have died are still linked to us in such a way that we can continue to communicate, to talk, with them. It is to believe that our relationship with them can continue to grow and that the reconciliation which, for many human reasons, was not possible in this life can now take place.

Why? Because not only is there communication between us and those who have died before us (this is the stuff of Christian doctrine, not that of séance) but because this com-munication is now privileged. Death washes clean. Not only does the church teach us that, we simply experience it.

How often in a family, in a friendship, in a community, in any human network, is there tension, misunderstanding, anger, frustration, irreconcilable difference, selfishness that divides, hurt which can no longer be undone, and then—

someone dies. The death brings with it a peace, a clarity and a charity which, prior to it, were not possible.

Why is this so? It is not because the death has changed the chemistry of the family or the office or the circle, nor because, as may sometimes seem the case, the source of the tension or headache or heartache or bitterness has died. It happens because, as Luke teaches us, when, on the cross Christ forgives the good thief, death washes things clean.

In the communion of saints we have privileged communication with those with whom we still have unfinished business. It can be a great consolation to die a happy death, snug and reconciled in the arms and the warm thoughts of those around us. Fortunately, for them and their loved ones, there is a privileged time after death to finish off some things for those whose lives end in situations full of bitterness, anger, irresponsibility, sin and lack of warmth and love.

A Showdown with True Love

AS A CHILD, raised on the old catechisms, I was taught to believe in purgatory. In that concept, after death you went to heaven, hell or purgatory. Heaven and hell were final. Once there, you went nowhere else. Purgatory was a transition state, a place separate from heaven.

It was understood to be a place of very intense suffering. We were constantly reminded to pray for the souls in purgatory. Suffering there was nearly as intense as in hell itself. However, unlike hell, purgatory was not permanent and the pains suffered there were purifying and not further embittering.

This belief was specifically Roman Catholic. For Protestants there was no intermediate place between heaven and hell.

Today many persons, Protestant and Roman Catholic alike, are benignly indifferent to the question of purgatory. It is seen as a remnant of an older system of thought that is not scripturally based and that has nothing vital to say about our relationship to God and each other.

Occasionally, though with an increasing rarity, one still hears the question: "Does purgatory still exist?" Purgatory does exist, not because it is dogmatically nailed down in Scripture but because it is impossible to formulate a science of love and community without it. Likewise it is impossible to speak of the paschal mystery without mention of purgatory.

But these statements imply a certain understanding of what purgatory is.

Purgatory is a stage of loving, the initial pain of entering into community. Mystics have classically defined purgatory as the pain of letting go of a lesser love and life in order to accept a deeper love and life. What is interesting in that definition is that purgatory is *not* a place separate from heaven, a place you go to in order to be punished for your sins so as to prepare you for heaven. *Purgatory is the pain of entering heaven.*

This can best be explained by way of an example. A young man came to see me. At the time he was also seeing a psychologist who in fact had sent him to me, a priest, to help deal with some of his guilt. His guilt centered around his past life and had been triggered by his falling in love. He was in his mid-twenties and had, more than a year before, become engaged to a young lady whom he deeply loved and who deeply loved him. She was an attractive and exceptionally good lady. She was his first serious love—and his first moral love.

In the four or five years prior to meeting her he had lived irresponsibly.

Although he had a good family background, during his university years he had drifted away from the church, from prayer and from the teaching on sexuality. During this period he had lived primarily by the pleasure principle.

What is curious is that during this irresponsibility his threshold of inner conflict and pain was minimal. He had been self-confident, cocky, seemingly without excess anxiety, solidly convinced of his own goodness and not particularly given to guilt.

That self-confident world collapsed soon after he fell in love. In love with a very good and moral person, he became aware of himself in a new way. Initially he simply felt guilty about his past sexual affairs, disappointed that in the light of meeting and falling in love with such a beautiful person he had not previously been faithful to that relationship. Eventually his inner conflict became more encompassing.

To his credit he sensed that he needed help to deal with this. He postponed plans to marry until, as he put it, he could get a better grip on his own selfishness and could work through some of his past and his guilts.

What seemed strange at the time was why he should be in such pain now, just when he had so beautifully fallen in love. But his pain was necessary, purgative and redemptively produced by the love itself.

Her love was saving him. It was a light that was showing him the dark corners of himself and it was also a power that was enabling him to face that darkness. This is the experience of grace.

Grace is eventually ecstatic, but initially it can be literally as painful as hell.

Purgatory, as this story illustrates, is the redemptive pain that follows falling in love. It is not an arbitrary punishment for sin. It is the pain of entering community.

The pattern of love, community and salvation is not *loneliness-falling-in-love-ecstasy*, but *loneliness-falling-in-love-a-brief-taste-of-ecstasy—a long, painful conflictual purgative experience-ecstasy.*

Morris West has remarked that: "All miracles begin with the act of falling in love." Salvation begins there. Purgatory sits between initial and final salvation.

Keep Praying for the Dead

G. K. CHESTERTON commented that tradition might be defined as an extension of the franchise. It gives a vote to the most obscure of all classes, the dead.

It is a democracy that includes the dead. Tradition refuses to submit to the small and arrogant oligarchy of those who merely happen to be walking around.

All people who believe in equality object to certain persons being disqualified by accident of birth; tradition objects to their being disqualified by accident of death.

A lady wrote asking me to write to her aunt and explain the Christian teaching about the communion of saints and prayers for the dead. Her aunt's son had been killed in an accident, and she had been dissuaded from having masses said for him. The question was: Can we still pray for the dead?

Well, if Chesterton is correct, and Christianity submits that he is, then we need to extend the franchise, we need to pray for the dead, both through liturgy and through private prayer.

Why? What possible good can it do? Looked at from a certain point of view, prayer for the dead can seem silly and superfluous. Why pray for the dead? To remind God to be merciful? God does not need reminders. To point out to God that our loved one who died was not so bad? God knows that.

God is already as merciful as love allows, and already

loves and understands our deceased loved one infinitely more deeply than we do.

As a student of mine once cynically put it: "If the person we are praying for is in hell then we can't help them, and if they are in heaven then they don't need help!"

So why pray for the dead?

For the same reason that we pray at all: we simply need to. The criticisms raised against praying for the dead might be used with equal logic against all prayer. God already knows everything, there is no need to remind God of anything. Yet God has asked us to pray, to pray always in fact.

Prayer, as we know, is not meant to change God's heart, but ours. Thus the first reason that we need to pray for the dead is because this prayer helps us, the living. We pray for the dead that, among other things, those of us left behind might be consoled. Tied to this, we pray for the dead to assuage our own guilt about continuing to live while the other died, and about our less-than-perfect relationship with the deceased. In praying for the dead many of the shortcomings we had in relating to them are washed clean.

We pray for them because, as we believe in the doctrine of the communion of saints, there is still a vital flow of life between them and ourselves. Love, presence and communication reach through death. We, and they, are still in one community of life. In a real way we can still feel each other's hearts.

Hence we pray for the dead to remain in communication with them. Just as we can hold someone's hand when they are dying, and this can be an immense consolation to them, so too, figuratively but really, we can hold a person's hand beyond death.

And now, much more than when they were alive, our communication is washed clean, the understanding is deeper, the forgiveness can be total, the perspective is wider, the anger and the shortcomings are unimportant. Communication with the dead is privileged, it undercuts so much of what kept us apart.

This, we believe, not only consoles us but also offers real strength and encouragement to the dead person. How? In the same way as loving presence to each other offers strength and consolation here in this life.

Imagine a young child learning how to swim. The child's mother and family cannot learn for the child, but if they are present and offering encouragement the struggle and learning are easier. Art Schopenhauer remarked: "Anything can be borne, if it can be shared."

By praying for the dead we share with them the adjustment to a new life (which includes the pain of letting go of this life). In our prayers for the dead, we offer encouragement and love to them as they, just born from the womb of the earth, adjust to a new life.

Classically we said that, for a while, our loved ones who die go to purgatory. That is true, though purgatory should not be understood as a place distinct from heaven. It is rather the pain of entering heaven and of being embraced by perfect love when we ourselves are less than perfect. Love itself can be a painful experience.

From my own experience of losing my parents and others I loved deeply, as well as from what others have shared with me, I have found that usually, after a time, we sense that we no longer need to pray for our loved ones who have died. Now we just talk with them.

What was for a time a cold, hurting absence becomes a warm presence. They are still with us.

In Much Better Hands Than Ours

I ATTENDED the funeral of a young man, a relative of mine, who had been killed in an automobile accident. He was eighteen, had graduated from high school and was just beginning adult life. A death like his is hard.

How does one begin the impossible task of understanding such an accident? What words, if any, have use as consolation?

When someone is struck down when life is really just beginning, words about resurrection and eternal life can sound hollow. A compulsory disconsolateness takes over. One can only, as the author of Lamentations puts it, put one's mouth to the dust and wait.

Later, after some time and healing, words about resurrection and fuller life can begin to take on more meaning.

Perhaps it is best not to speak too much at funerals. Our stuttering and inarticulateness perhaps say what needs to be said: "I am here. I care. I'll suffer with you; but, for now, there is nothing that can be said!"

And yet there is a need for some words which help clarify our relationship to the person we are burying and to the God we believe in.

When someone close to us dies, especially a young person, we experience more than simple shock and hurt. We are left as well with feelings of guilt and fear. At one level we feel guilty because we go on living while someone else dies. At another level, a more painful one, we feel guilty about the in-completeness of our relationship with the person who has died, even if that relationship was essentially a good one.

There is a painful incompleteness in all relationships and nowhere is this more felt than at funerals. When someone dies, immediately there is a guilt. There is the feeling that, given more time, we could have had a more complete rela-tionship, affection could have been expressed more deeply, a more complete understanding and reconciliation could have been achieved. Now everything seems frozen in this state of incompleteness.

Coupled with this, especially if the one who died was young, there are feelings of fear and anxiety. We sense an un-finishedness, an unreadiness and even a certain brutality: "He was so young, so fragile still, so unprepared to give up life and to be so finally separated from home and friends, to be made to face the judgment of an eternity that he didn't have full time to prepare for."

Like a mother who worries about her child when she or he first leaves home, we worry about the young who die. They are too tender still to be subjected to death, to irrevoca-ble separation, to a terrifying newness, to a final judgment.

Acceptance of the death of the young comes hard. Understanding comes harder still.

As we search among the strands of hope and grasp for something to hang on to in the face of such a death, perhaps we can do no better than to seize on to the words: *He is in better hands than ours*.

Those are words of faith and they assure us that the God who gave this young man life, who gave him a gentle mother, a loving family and friends, who gave him exuberance and the lively life of the young, can be further trusted to bring that life to completeness and to bring him gently into life everlasting.

In understanding death, it is useful to look at birth. When a child is born, she or he is born into the arms and care of a mother. Save for the tremendous care, gentleness and attention of a mother, a child is radically unready to live in this world.

Given a mother, everything changes. There is some trauma in being born, but it is brief. Very quickly the gentleness, patience and tenderness of a mother erase the trauma of birth.

In the care of a loving mother, the passage from birth to adulthood is not ungentle and traumatic, but a delightful adventure in awakening.

God is our real mother—more tender, more loving and more understanding than any earthly mother. Our birth into eternal life through the birth canal of death must be seen just as our birth into this life. Without a mother the trauma would be too much. Given a mother, everything changes.

Just as here, in infancy, our mother was ever tender and patient with us, in death, even more so is God. The hands that receive us at death are not the rough hands of our world. The heart that embraces us there will not let anything be too much for us. We will, children that we are, be gently, understandingly and tenderly guided and coaxed into eternal life. Being born into God's arms will surely be as gentle and tender an experience as being born into our mother's arms.

Doubtless there will always be guilt and fear when people close to us die. Death takes our loved ones away with a finality that nothing in this life will ever match. But in this parting we are saved the biggest worry of all.

When people leave us in this life to move on to new places and new things, we have no assurance as to what they might be falling into. When they leave us in death, we have such an assurance: *They are in better, and infinitely more gentle, hands than ours!*

The Death of a Soldier

ONE OF THE MOST PRECIOUS of all experiences is being with a person when he or she is dying. Paradoxically, death clarifies so many things about life and the dying often generate community in ways that the living cannot.

A group of us were with a young American soldier as he died. That group was a curious mixture: a commanding officer with no church affiliation, an agnostic American doctor, two German doctors (of whose backgrounds I know nothing), a young American couple and myself, a Catholic priest. We were all there, for different reasons, to watch Sgt. Mark die.

Mark had been fatally injured in an accident two days previously and was being sustained by life-support machines. The German doctors now decided to unhook those machines since there was no longer any brain function and, according to German law, a person is then legally dead. His parents had been telephoned and had reluctantly consented to have the machines removed. They requested three things: that a Catholic priest be present, that an American doctor verified that Mark's condition was truly hopeless, and that Mark's closest friend, a fellow GI in Germany, was present.

The commanding officer gathered us and we met in his car en route to the hospital. It was awkward and strained. We were meeting each other for the first time, the situation itself was sufficiently tense, and we were very different kinds of persons.

The commanding officer was used to commanding and his attitudes and clothing showed it. The doctor was all business, talking of tests and legalities. Mark's friends, Danny and his wife Patty, were in sharp contrast, simple folk casually dressed, religious and pious, down-to-earth and very scared, praying and crying. However they would soon enough show a courage which would help us all.

I was the unknown priest summoned for the occasion, not used to commanding officers or watching life-support systems being turned off; also scared and praying.

We arrived at the hospital where Mark lay: a boy of twenty-two in a foreign country, without his family, soon to die.

The American doctor grimly checked the tests and retained that grimness as he nodded to the German doctors and to us. The German doctors approached me: "*Jetzt*— should we do it now?"

I looked at Danny and Patty and we asked for some time to pray. The three doctors and the officer stood back. I clutched the book of rites and led prayers for the dying. Danny clutched Patty with one hand and Mark's near lifeless hand with his other and we prayed as we had seldom prayed before: the prayers for the dying, the Lord's Prayer, some Hail Marys.

When we finished Danny, a tall man (six feet five inches—most of it honest heart), put his head on Mark's chest. He began to cry.

I nodded to the German doctors, all business in their medical uniforms. Four or five turns of a valve and the machines stopped. It was as simple as turning off a heating radiator.

When it was over Danny's tears stopped. Releasing Mark's hand he stood tall and pounded Mark's chest: "Sgt.

Mark, congratulations! You are the first of all of us to make it home! Goodbye!" He spoke the words loudly, with strength. Afterward we walked from the room.

Outside, through a glass paneling, we saw the German doctors slowly removing the machines and tubes. Danny, Patty and I stopped for a last few Hail Marys.

Then we hugged each other, dried tears and walked to the waiting room where we sat to compose ourselves and to wait for the officer and the American doctor to finish signing forms.

There was a different atmosphere en route home. The commanding officer was less commanding, his tie was loosened considerably and so was his heart. The doctor now talked no more of tests and legalities, for we all talked of meaning and purpose in life.

Danny and Patty no longer looked out of place in their denims. They clutched each other's hands and the rest of us regretted only that for the sake of pride and proper appearance we were prevented from joining hands as well.

I was no longer awkward or scared, and it felt oh, so good to be a priest!

There we sat, strangers, though not quite anymore, all so different, but now bound warmly because of what we had shared. Yes, we sat now, seeing life and each other with a clarity and charity seldom given.

We had prayed for Mark and those prayers, I am sure, had helped him. But they had also helped us. It was a rare grace.

Congratulations, Sgt. Mark!

Hope at the Time of Death

I RECEIVED THE NEWS that a close friend of our family was killed in an industrial accident. Nothing prepares you for that kind of news. Since the phone rang I have prayed. I have prayed for the victim, for his family and loved ones, and I have prayed for faith and hope and for the wisdom to know what to say when I speak at this man's funeral.

What does one say in the face of a death of this kind? What feeble lifeline of consolation can be clung to for perspective and courage? In what words lie the seeds of courage?

We have the words of our faith: "He is in God's hands! We believe in the resurrection and in life everlasting! Life is changed not ended! Here we have no lasting city, we are pilgrims destined for an eternal city!" Rich words, true words, but when spoken in the face of actual death they offer perhaps only an anemic consolation. They can be said too easily.

What can be said? Perhaps nothing should be said at all. To the extent that we have faith, we already know God cares, that our final hope lies beyond this life and that we are destined for resurrection. To the extent that we do not have faith, all words are inadequate to offer hope at the time of death.

Perhaps the consolation and courage we seek at a time like this are found not in words, but in a simple presence to each other, in the simple gesture of hugging and silently sharing pain and helplessness. Perhaps that says all that needs to be said: "I am here. I care. There is nothing I can say to make things better. I know you do not expect me to say anything!"

Perhaps in our stuttering and awkward inability to say anything meaningful, in the helpless silence and pointless small talk, lie the compassion that makes the lifeline through which the nurturing milk of consolation and hope can flow back and forth.

I think that is true. The deepest consolation we can offer each other lies in sharing helplessness. Too much is said at funerals. There is a need for fewer words.

But beyond this there is a need for some speaking, for words which can clarify our relationship to the dead person and to each other, for words which can stimulate courage and faith, and for words which can help us celebrate that courage and faith.

What words should be shared at the time of death of a loved one?

Words that tell us that our hope lies in love, and not primarily in biological life. Psychologist John Powell submits that there are only two potential tragedies in life, and dying young is not one of them.

These are the two potential tragedies: if we go through life and we do not love fully, and if we go through life and do not tell those we love that we love them.

In the face of death, our own death or that of a loved one, there is always deep regret. But this is not a regret which focuses on the sins and shortcomings of our lives and makes us fear eternal punishment. No. The regret is that so much love has been unlived, unexpressed, unappreciated, badly received and left unreconciled. In the face of death the deepest yearning is for more time for reconciliation, more time to express love fully.

When we speak to each other at the time of a death our words should express this. They should convey that death challenges us not to become morose, more withdrawn from life. Rather death challenges us to enter life more deeply in love, appreciation and especially in reconciliation.

In the world, worse things can befall one than death. Christ warned of this when he said: "What does it profit one to gain the whole world and suffer the loss of one's soul?" The loss he talked about is the loss of concern, the loss of conscience, the loss of one's love for others, the loss of the hope of reconciliation.

These can be snuffed out by a different kind of death, a bitterness or a selfishness or a dishonesty which kills compassion. When a person dies, if conscience, love and the desire for reconciliation remain, nothing is lost.

I stood at the bedside of a young lady, Cathy, who was dying of cancer. She looked at us through tears and said: "This is hard, but I am not bitter, so it's OK!" She died. New hope was born in us. Her few words were enough. We knew that nothing had been lost.

Words need also to be spoken to alleviate our guilt, the guilt of those of us who are not dying. Whenever someone close to us dies we struggle through a deep guilt. Somehow we feel responsible and we think of the hundreds of things we could and should have done before it was too late.

We need to be reminded that God loves that person more than we do. God has his own way of writing straight with the crooked lines we have made. He has his own way of bringing this person's partially frustrated life to fulfillment.

God understands that given human nature, accidents, illness, complexity and sin we will always be inadequate. We do our best. For God, in faith, it is enough.

Our God is understanding, compassionate and powerful.

Our life is eternal. We need to celebrate this, especially in the face of death. Like Cathy, we need to look at each other through our tears and say: "This is hard, but we're not bitter, so it's OK!"

Love, conscience, shared life, the desire for reconciliation, in these lie life and hope. A man has died; none of these has been lost.

13

IT IS NOT GOOD TO BE ALONE: COMMUNITY AND THE CHURCH

The discipline of community frees us to go wherever the spirit guides us, even to places we would rather not go. This is the real pentecost experience.

(HENRI NOUWEN)

Community—Our Greatest Need

I GREW UP IN A CHURCH which was concerned with apologetics. We were forever worried about making ourselves credible. A lot of effort went into showing that the faith made sense, that being a Christian fulfilled rather than denigrated humanity. We devised all kinds of arguments intended to impress or discredit non-believers: proofs for the existence of God, arguments demonstrating why the human person needs God, and schemata that tried to demonstrate the validity of the church as an institution.

As a young man studying theology I often met this kind of question in a classroom: "Imagine you are traveling on a bus and you meet an atheist, how would you talk about God to such a person?"

Or for those of us who were Roman Catholics, "Imagine you are on a train and meet a Protestant, how would you attempt to show that the Roman Catholic Church is the right one?"

Most of these arguments did not get beyond the safety of the classroom. I have been in ministry for fifteen years and have rarely, on bus, train, boat or plane, met that questioning atheist or Protestant. Most talk on buses and trains revolves around sports, entertainment, politics and food.

Despite this the old apologetics had some value, it helped make the faith more credible to those within it.

We still need an apologetics. However its audience has radically changed. If I wrote or taught on apologetics today I would pose the question this way: "Imagine you are sitting at your family table, where some of your own family no longer attend church or take seriously the church's moral teachings, how would you try to prove that faith and Christianity are credible?" We have come a long way from the theoretical atheist on the bus!

The problem of faith in our time is the problem of unbelief among believers. For too many of us faith in Christ is little more than a hangover, toxic residue from a former activity.

What do I perceive as the issue behind this?

The problem, I submit, both within and without, is a problem of credibility, the faith is no longer believable or livable for many in our age.

Why? Why is Christ known, but not really believed in?

When I scan religious literature I see various proposed explanations. Conservatives blame our present malaise upon lack of prayer and the failure of our age to keep the commandments, pure and simple. If we do not pray and our moral lives are shabby, how can we expect to have a vital faith?

Liberals point to slow renewal within the church as the cause. We are not really renewed, they argue. We still pray to God, talk about God, and worship God in mythical and medieval images.

We are schizophrenic in regard to religion. We live modern lives but try to live an old-time religion. Ultimately this freezes God out of all the important areas of life. Religion becomes the great art form and the church becomes the great museum.

Social justice advocates submit that the problem is one of affluence. If Christ made a preferential option for the poor and Christianity is seeing life from the bottom, it is, quite simply, impossible to live as affluently and selfishly as we do and still have a vital connection to Christ.

There is some truth in each of these, but in the end the real reason for the erosion of faith and hope in Christ is something beyond them all.

What, singularly, are we missing today within Christianity that could make us credible to the world and to our own families? Community. The greatest need in our time is, as Jim Wallis puts it:

> not simply for kerygma, the preaching of the Gospel; nor for diakonia, service on behalf of justice; nor for charisma, the experience of the spirit's gifts; nor even for propheteia, the challenging of the King. The greatest need of our time is for koinonia, the call simply to be church . . . to offer to the world a living, breathing, loving community of church. This is the foundation of all answers. (Jim Wallis, *The Call to Conversion*, Lion, 1982)

In the end people are as agnostic about faith, Christ and the church as they are about the experience of community. When there is a strong experience of community there is generally a strong faith. For example, wherever today we see a strong faith we see, invariably, strong community—RCIA groups, cursillo groups, marriage encounter groups, social justice groups, charismatic groups, Bible study groups, third order groups. These are pockets of fervor within the church and it is no accident that all of them are linked to strong community experiences.

As well, even in those Christians who are deeply committed and beyond first fervor, we see that ultimately their strength issues from community, the Eucharist, common prayer and a shared morality and life within the Holy Spirit.

Christianity, in the end, is a communal endeavor. We believe in it when community works, we stop believing in it when community and family break down.

Our primary task today is to live community. If we can do that, then the visible body of Christ, the church, will have an incredible resurrection.

Crying Out for Real Community

I CLIPPED A LETTER out of a magazine. A lady was explaining why she had trouble accepting the Christian faith. She wrote:

> Do not talk to me of God or come to my door with tracts or stop me in the street to ask if I am saved. Hell holds no threat more agonizing than the harsh reality of my life. I swear to you the fires of hell seem more inviting than this bone-deep cold of my existence.
>
> Neither speak to me of church. What does the church know of my despair, the church barricaded behind its stained-glass windows against the likes of me? Once I heard your pleas for my repentance and sought a fellowship of faith within your walls.
>
> There I saw your God reflected in your faces as you turned away . . . Forgiveness never came . . . The healing love I sought was carefully hoarded, reserved only for your kind.
>
> Be gone from me and speak no more of God. I've seen your God made manifest in you: a God with no compassion. So long as your God withholds the warmth of human touch from me I shall remain an unbeliever. (Marie Livingston Roy)

Wisdom lies in simplicity. This letter is powerful because it is simple. When we do not experience the warmth of human touch, in the end we will not believe the Gospel.

This is so true that, ultimately, we cannot even honestly preach the Gospel when we cannot offer community to those to whom we are preaching.

I say we cannot preach it honestly, not because people might look at lack of community in our own lives and say, "You aren't practicing what you are preaching," but because, when we cannot offer community to people, we put them into a position where, by hearing the Gospel, they find themselves in an intolerable but hopeless situation. The Gospel challenges them to leave one life behind but does not offer a concrete road to a new life.

When we preach and teach like that, and we are all prone to, we end up like the scribes and pharisees of Scripture, laying all kinds of burdens upon people, with the word of God, and not being of any value in setting them free for new life.

Let me illustrate this.

When the rich young man asks Jesus, "What must I do to gain eternal life?" Jesus answers, "Sell all you have, give the money to the poor, and come and follow me." However, when Jesus says, "Come and follow me," this expression, literally, means: "Come and move in with us, be part of our community."

Jesus challenged the young man to give up everything, but he offered him immediately an alternative life within his community.

Today, for most of us, when we preach we cannot offer this kind of alternative. Hence our preaching can be dishonest.

For example, suppose that after a homily on social justice a man approached me and said: "I am convinced. I will go today and sell everything, give the money to the poor, and follow Christ in a more radical way. But, then, afterward, what should I do? How should I then support my family?"

I would have no answer. I could not tell him, as Jesus did, "Come move in with us!" I could not, concretely, offer him a community that would absorb and support him and his family. Hence my original homily on social justice contains an element of dishonesty. I am challenging but not offering a real alternative. I am making him feel guilty but not offering a way out.

This holds true for a lot of our preaching; for example sexual ethics.

Recently I was talking with a lady in her late thirties. She is, in her own way, a sincere and committed Catholic. However because she is unmarried, lonely and unable to find deep faith, emotional and affective support, she is prone to sexual affairs. She in no way justifies these morally, but she does justify them emotionally.

Simply put, she knows they are a compensation, something second-best. But, as she puts it: "Right now, where I am at—lonely, single, frustrated sexually, envious of those who are happily married and have children—these kind of affairs are a compensation for all I don't have. They are better than nothing!"

It is hard to challenge her on this, without being able to offer her, concretely, a community of persons who could provide for her something of the emotional, affective and faith support that she needs to be strong enough not to fall into that kind of relationship.

Like the rich young man in Scripture, she often walks away sad, both from her affairs and from a Christ she knows at a deeper and truer level inside herself. However her guilt is less than the rich young man's.

Nobody and no community which is truly representative of Christ has ever yet said to her: "Leave it all behind—and come, move in with us!"

Christianity will have power when we have vital communities which can, concretely, offer an alternative to the second-best compensations that our world offers.

When the touch of human warmth, genuine community, is withheld, we will always have a lot of unbelievers and a lot of struggling believers.

Can You Ever Really Leave Home?

SEVERAL YEARS AGO Carlo Carretto, one of the great spiritual writers of our time, returned to Italy from the Sahara desert after many years as a monk among the Bedouin. He then wrote a spiritual testimony, *I Sought and I Found* (DLT, 1984), within which he chronicles his journey toward, and struggles with, God.

He ends the book with a letter, a love letter, addressed to the church, the visible institutional church.

A paraphrase of the opening lines reads like this:

How much I must criticize you, my church and yet how much I love you!

You have made me suffer more than anyone and yet I owe you more than I owe anyone.

I should like to see you destroyed and yet I need your presence.

You have given me much scandal and yet you alone have made me understand holiness.

Never in the world have I seen anything more obscurantist, more compromised, more false, yet never have I touched anything more pure, more generous or more beautiful.

Countless times I have felt like slamming the door of my soul in your face—and yet, every night, I have prayed that I might die in your sure arms!

No, I cannot be free of you, for I am one with you, even if not completely you.

Then too—where should I go?

To build another church?

But I cannot build another church without the same defects, for they are my own defects. And again, if I were to build another church, it would be my church, not Christ's church.

No. I am old enough. I know better!

What a magnificent description of the church—flawed yet divine, mediating God's presence even as it obstructs it!

I have found myself drawing upon this description more and more as I deal with complaints about the institutional church.

What is to be said in the face of the fact that the institutional church is flawed, compromised, corrupted by power, fraught with human weakness and pettiness?

What is to be said in the face of the fact that the church has never lived radically and fully the Gospel it preaches?

What is to be said in the face of the fact that, in its darker moments, the church has hurt, and continues to hurt, countless persons? How can it claim credibility and how can it claim to mediate God's presence in the light of this?

These are frequently voiced complaints and often one hears the added comment: "I can deal with God, I can't deal with the church!"

Such complaints are often sincere, though they can also be a rationalization. In either case, however, the facts they point to are true. We cannot deny history and reality. The church has always had, and still has, a dark side. It does not mediate God's presence purely. That is simply a fact.

However, with that having been admitted, something else must be added. The church, just as humanity itself, is not something abstract. It exists only in real people. We meet the church only in a very particular, historical, concrete enflesh-ment, that is, in real people with real names, real problems and real blemishes. What we meet is never the church, but only this or that particular church.

The church is a family, a very concrete and historical one.

This can be, I feel, a helpful perspective to keep in mind. When we are born into a family we bear its birthmark. We can dislike it, we can get angry with it, we can stay away from family celebrations for long periods, we can rage against its faults, and we can fill with bitterness and protest that it should be more loving, more understanding, less quick to judge and assign guilt—but in the end it is our family and we want to die reconciled with it.

Ultimately one of life's non-negotiable imperatives is that one tries to come to peace with one's family. Nobody ever really leaves one's family, even if they die outside of it.

It is the same with the institutional church. It is not God. The institutional church is no more identifiable with God than my historical father is identifiable with God the Father. But, like our historical parents, it is real, it is what we actu-ally meet on earth.

As with our real family, we can dislike it, rage at its faults, and be bitter about its imperfections. We can wish for another family. We can fight with it and stay away for long periods (and sometimes this can be healthy), but in the end we bear its mark on our skin, it is ours, it is the actual and only place in history where we contact the historical Christ.

It is because of this, its inexorable reality, that we have

such strong feelings about it. Like Carretto, there are the times when we feel like slamming the door of our soul into its face, and yet, daily, we pray somehow to die in its arms.

It is because of this that, like Carretto, we too ultimately realize that we can never really leave the church.

EPILOGUE

COMMANDMENTS FOR THE LONG HAUL

Reality might not be all it's cracked up to be, but it's still the only place you can get a decent steak.

(Woody Allen)

Some of Life's Questions

RARELY DO FAITH, hope and love come to us pure. Instead, like life itself, they come with mess and doubt, raising huge questions.

Living a human life is not a simple business, especially if one attempts to do this beyond simple instinct. To try to believe in something beyond sight and understanding, to try to place one's trust in something beyond what one can secure, and to try to love non-manipulatively not infrequently raises more questions than it answers.

Not to be haunted by doubt, ambiguity and temptation is to close oneself off from deep thought and feeling. To think and to feel is to be open to many things, darkness as well as light, hatred as well as love, despair as much as hope.

Maurice Merleau-Ponty, the great philosopher of phenomenology, based an entire philosophy on the dictum: Ambiguity is the fundamental fact within experience. That is the philosopher's way of saying that it is not simple out there, that our heads and hearts are full of too many things, and that life is mostly about sorting things out.

And sorting things out is seldom easy. Many voices inside and around us beckon with their own truth—instinctual truth, higher truth, head truth, heart truth, Christian truth, yuppie truth, economic truth, spiritual truth—what is truth?

Which voice speaks truth when so many voices vie with each other? We are called in every direction.

Deep inside us the call is to be a saint, to believe that meaning and happiness lie in generosity and self-forgetfulness; yet other voices, also deep inside us, demand other things, they would have us experience every sensation of the sinner, securing things for ourselves, building a name and a nest.

Which of these voices speaks truth? Does the truth lie in gratitude? Bitterness? Trust? Paranoia? The voices contradict each other and yet each holds its own promise of life, rest, realism, meaning. Small wonder that living can become a tiring enterprise!

So life has its questions. As we struggle to love each other, what is real?

Is the distance between us expanding or is it shrinking?

Are we touching each other's neuroses, or depth?

Are we falling ever more into despair, or is it love?

Do we say the same words too often, or not often enough?

Are we bonded to each other by neurotic pain-giving, or by painful life-giving?

In our obsessions are we bewailing a universal inconsummation, or are we filling in what is lacking in the suffering of Christ?

In our often frayed emotions are we tasting hell, or are we experiencing birth pangs?

Do our frustrations in love unleash our deepest angers, or do they cauterize our worst sins?

Does love itself demand more distance from each other or does it need more mouth-to-mouth resuscitation?

Does passion turn love into idolatry, or into holy icon?

Is the pain of non-requited love the pain of hell or is it the pain of purgatory, which feels like hell when heaven cannot be touched?

Questions, love's questions, questions which pose other questions of faith and hope:

Can Christ be believed?

Does dying produce new life?

Does purgatory turn into heaven?

Can what does not seem to be real be, in the end, the most real?

Can spirit really triumph over instinct, heart over groin?

Can hope find the infinitely small gap through which the future can break into our lives in a new and marvelous way?

Can tombs be opened—and reopened—and reopened?

Do we really have seventy times seven chances?

Will the smell of fresh fish invariably greet us after a night of emptiness?

Can our wounds really turn into sure proofs of the resurrection, silencing our doubts as they silenced Thomas?

Can, when all the emotions, angers, obsessions, jealousies, insecurities and immaturities die down, love really last?

Can the ideal really take on flesh?

In the end, that is really the only question—and how we answer it will fundamentally fashion or distort us as human beings.

Guidelines for the Long Haul

SEVERAL YEARS AGO Daniel Berrigan wrote *Ten Commandments for the Long Haul*. It offers advice on how to sustain ourselves until Christ returns.

Here, with the help of various authors, I too offer a few commandments designed to help us during the long haul:

BE GRATEFUL: NEVER LOOK A GIFT UNIVERSE IN THE MOUTH!

To be a saint is nothing less than to be warmed and vitalized by gratitude. We owe it to our Creator to appreciate things, to be as happy as we can. Pay for a lovely moment by enjoying it. Resist pessimism and false guilt.

Add this section to the Lord's Prayer: "Give us today our daily bread, and help us to enjoy it without guilt." Keep God central in all.

DON'T BE NAÏVE ABOUT GOD: SHE OR HE WILL SETTLE FOR NOT LESS THAN EVERYTHING!

Distrust all talk about the consolation of religion. Religion puts a belt around you and takes you to where you would rather not be. Get used to virtue; it gives you a constant reminder of what you have missed out on.

Know that God will settle for not less than everything. Demands from God always seem unreasonable. Learn to wrestle with God; you can win, by losing.

WALK FORWARD WHEN POSSIBLE: WHEN IMPOSSIBLE, TRY TO GET ONE FOOT IN FRONT OF THE NEXT!

Expect long periods of darkness and confusion. Take to wonder. Take consolation in the fact that Jesus cried, saints sinned, Peter betrayed. See what you see, it is enough to walk by. Be stubborn as a mule; the only thing that shatters dreams is compromise.

Let ordinary life be enough. Start over often.

PRAY: THAT GOD WILL HANG ON TO YOU!

Distrust Gallup polls. Trust prayer. Prayer is an enlargement. Be willing to die a little to be with God. He is dying to be with us. Let your heart, as Henri Nouwen puts it, become the place where the tears of God and the tears of God's children merge and become the tears of hope.

LOVE: IF A LIFE IS LARGE ENOUGH FOR LOVE, IT IS LARGE ENOUGH!

Create a space for love in your life. Accept that nothing can be loved too much, though all things can be loved in the wrong way. Make love your eye. Say to those you love: "You, at least, shall not die!"

Know that there are only two potential tragedies to life: not to love and not to tell those whom we love that we love them.

ACCEPT WHAT YOU ARE: FEAR NOT—
YOU ARE INADEQUATE!

Be just sufficiently fallible to be human. If you are weak
alone, without confidence and without answers, say so, then
listen. Accept the torture of a life that is inadequate.
Understand your own brand of martyrdom. If you die for a
good reason, it is something you can live with!

DON'T MUMMIFY:
LET GO, SO AS NOT TO BE PUSHED!

Accept daily deaths. Do not hold on to life as possession.
Possessiveness kills enjoyment. Let go of life gracefully. The
greatest strength of life is the power to resign it. Death-
corruption-resurrection, that is the true rhythm. Keep in
mind that it is difficult to distinguish a moment of dying
from a moment of birth.

REFUSE TO TAKE THINGS SERIOUSLY:
CALL YOURSELF A FOOL REGULARLY!

Laugh and play and give yourself over to silliness; these are (as
C. S. Lewis pointed out) a disgusting and direct insult to the realism, dignity and austerity of hell. Do not confuse sneering with
laughter. Keep in mind that it is easy to be heavy; hard to be light.

STAY WITH THE FOLKS:
YOU ARE ON A GROUP OUTING!

Do not journey alone. Be "born again" more fully into community. Accept that there are strings attached. To go any-

where in life we have to take along the family, the church, the country and the human race. Do not be seduced by the false lure of absolute freedom. Learn obedience to community—it humbles, deflates the ego, puts you into purgatory and then into heaven.

DON'T BE AFRAID TO GO SOFT: REDEMPTION LIES IN TEARS!

Resist the macho impulse; the person who will not have a softening of the heart will eventually have a softening of the brain.

As G. K. Chesterton put it: "The swiftest things are the softest things. A bird is active because a bird is soft. A stone is helpless because a stone is hard. The stone by its nature goes downward, because hardness is weakness. A bird can of its nature go upwards; fragility is force."

Know that there are two kinds of darkness one can enter: the fearful darkness of paranoia, which brings sadness, and the fetal darkness of conversion, which brings life.

Ronald Rolheiser, OMI, is the author of *The Holy Longing,* which has sold more than 150,000 copies, *The Restless Heart,* and *The Shattered Lantern.* He is a specialist in spirituality and systematic theology and writes a regular columm for the *Catholic Herald.* He lives in Toronto, Canada.

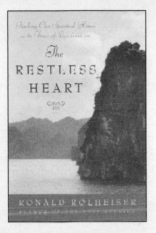